PIANO • VOCAL • GUITAR

TODAY'S WORSHIP HITS

T0082003

ISBN 978-1-4584-0537-1

HAL•LEONARD®
CORPORATION
7777 W. BLUEMOUND RD. P.O. BOX 13819 MILWAUKEE, WI 53213

Visit Hal Leonard Online at
www.halleonard.com

4	All Because of Jesus
12	Awesome Is the Lord Most High
19	Beautiful One
26	Christ Is Risen
32	Desert Song
45	Give Us Clean Hands
40	Glory to God Forever
50	God of This City
64	God You Reign
59	Happy Day
70	How Deep the Father's Love for Us
74	How He Loves
88	Indescribable
94	Jesus Paid It All
100	Let God Arise
106	The Lord Reigns
81	Majestic
121	Mighty to Save
114	A New Hallelujah
130	Our God
138	Our God Saves
145	Revelation Song
152	Sing, Sing, Sing
162	Sing to the King
166	Speak O Lord
170	Today Is the Day
178	You Alone Can Rescue
185	You Are God Alone (not a god)
194	You, You Are God
200	Your Love Never Fails

ALL BECAUSE OF JESUS

Words and Music by
STEVE FEE

Driving Rock beat

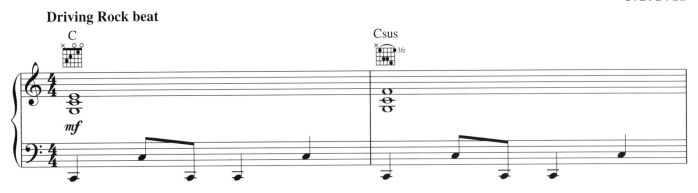

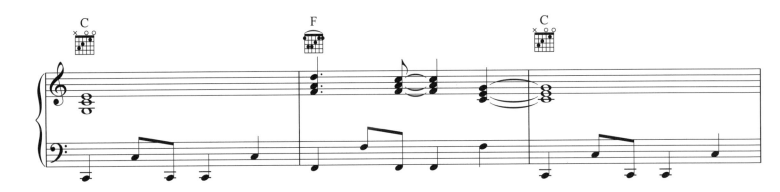

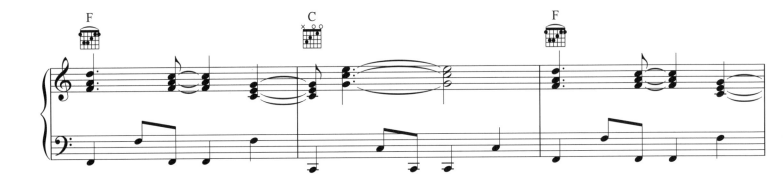

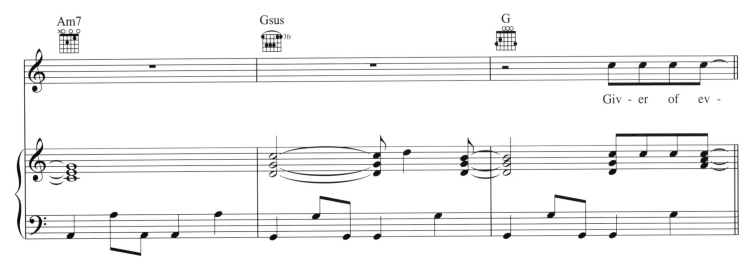

Giv - er of ev -

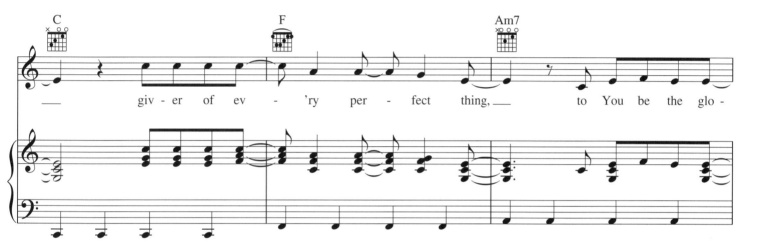

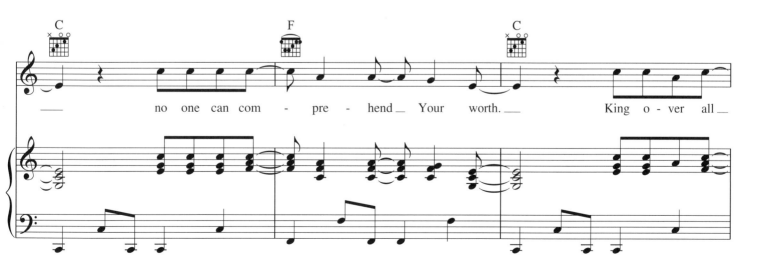

the u - ni - verse, ___ to You be the glo - ry.

And I am a - live ___ be - cause ___ I'm a - live ___ in You. ___

And it's all ___ be - cause ___ of Je -

- sus I'm ___ a - live. ___ Yeah, it's all ___ be - cause ___ the blood ___

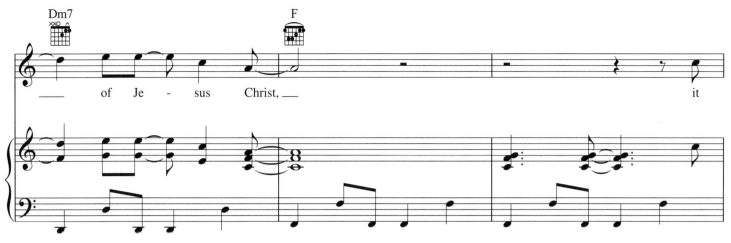

_of Je - sus Christ, ___ it

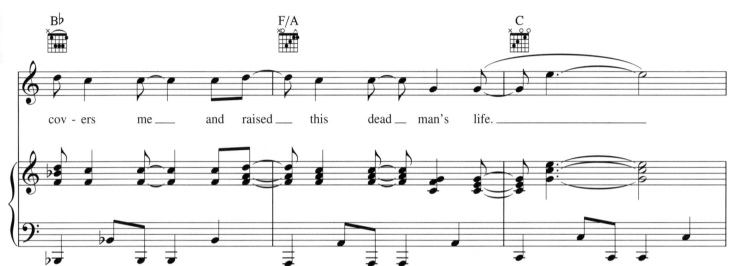

cov - ers me ___ and raised ___ this dead ___ man's life. ___

To Coda

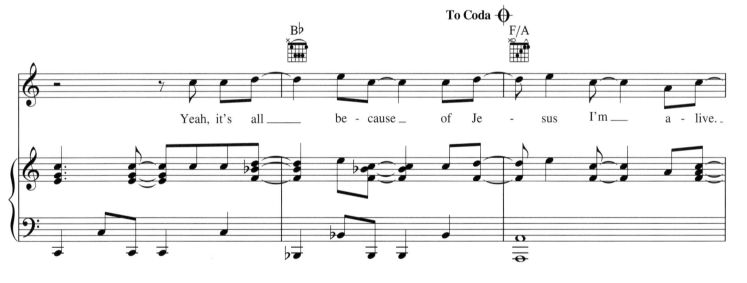

Yeah, it's all ___ be - cause ___ of Je - sus I'm ___ a - live.

I'm a - live, ___ I'm a - live. ___

D.S. al Coda

Giv - er of ev -

CODA

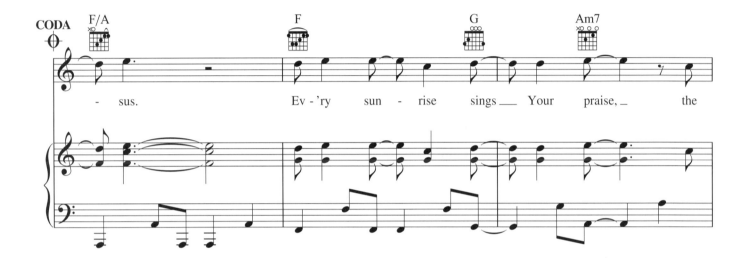

- sus. Ev - 'ry sun - rise sings ___ Your praise, ___ the

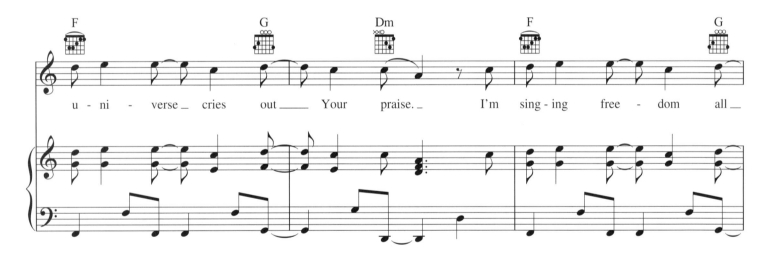

u - ni - verse ___ cries out ___ Your praise. ___ I'm sing - ing free - dom all ___

___ my days, ___ now that I'm ___ a - live. _____

It's all be - cause _ of Je - sus I'm _ a - live. _

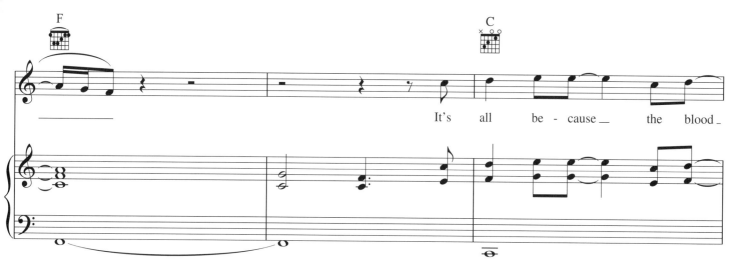

_ It's all be - cause _ the blood _

_ of Je - sus Christ, _ and it's all _

_ be - cause _ of Je - sus I'm _ a - live. _

Yeah, it's all ___ be - cause ___ the blood ___ of Je - sus Christ, ___

___ it cov - ers me ___ and raised ___

___ this dead ___ man's life. _____ Yeah, it's all ___

___ be - cause ___ of Je - sus I'm ___ a - live. ___

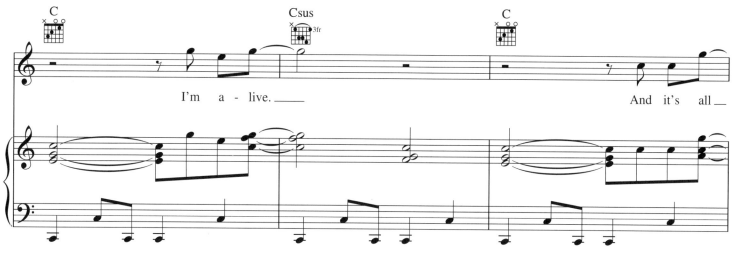

I'm a - live. _____ And it's all _____

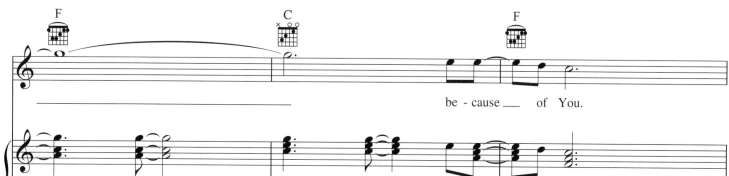

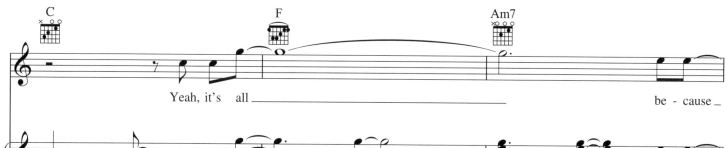

be - cause _____ of You.

Yeah, it's all _____ be - cause _

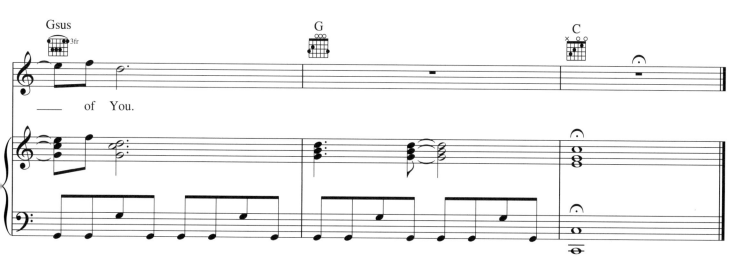

_____ of You.

AWESOME IS THE LORD MOST HIGH

Words and Music by CHRIS TOMLIN,
JESSE REEVES, CARY PIERCE
and JON ABEL

Moderately fast

Great are You, ___ Lord, ___
Where You send ___ us, ___

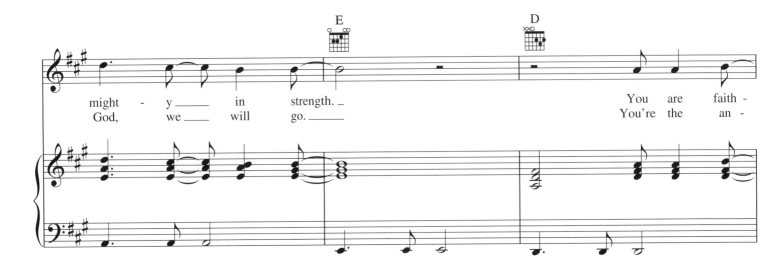

might - y ___ in strength. ___
God, we ___ will go. ___

You are faith-
You're the an -

-ful, and You will ev - er be. ___
-swer; we want the world ___ to know. ___

We will praise ___ You all of ___ our days. ___
We will trust ___ You when You call ___ our name. ___

___ It's for Your glo - ry we
___ Where You lead ___ us, we'll

of - fer ev - 'ry - thing. ___
fol - low all ___ the way. ___ Raise your hands, all you na -

-tions. Shout to God, all cre - a - tion. How

awe - some __ is the Lord Most __ High. _____

We will praise You to - geth-

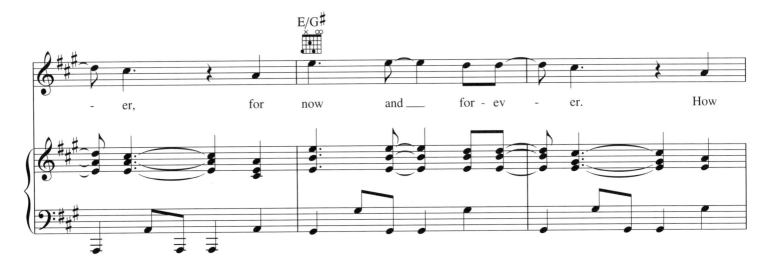

-er, for now and __ for - ev - er. How

awe - some __ is the Lord Most __ High. _____

Hal - le - lu - jah!

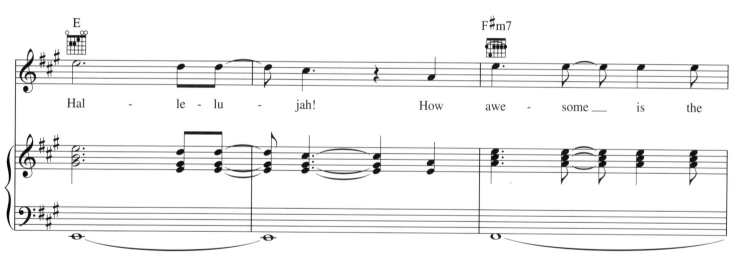

Hal - le - lu - jah! How awe - some __ is the

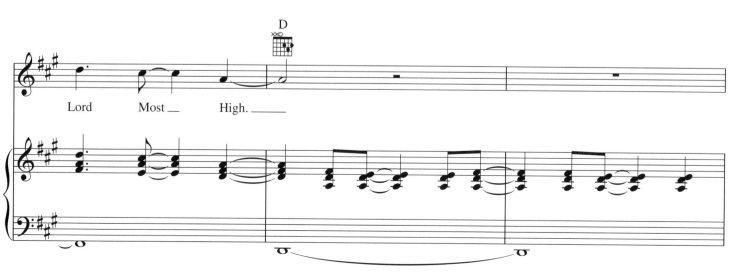

Lord Most __ High. _____

awe - some __ is the Lord Most __ High. _____

We will praise You to - geth - er, for

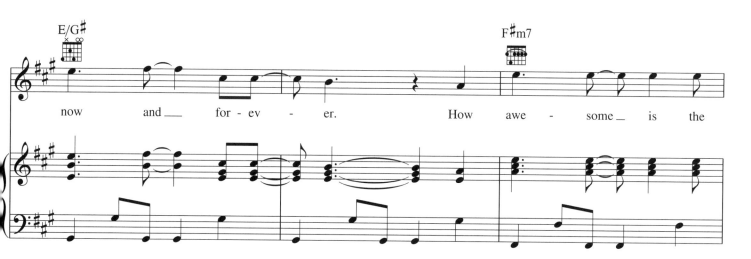

now and __ for - ev - er. How awe - some __ is the

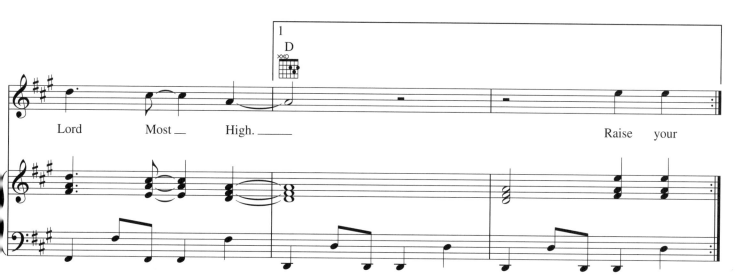

Lord Most __ High. _____ Raise your

The Lord Most _ High. _____
(Vocal 1st time only)

How

awe - some _ is the Lord Most _ High. _____

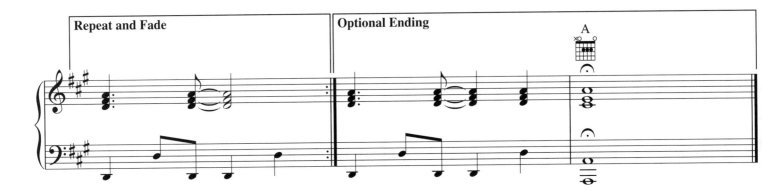

Repeat and Fade

Optional Ending

BEAUTIFUL ONE

Words and Music by
TIM HUGHES

Moderately fast Rock

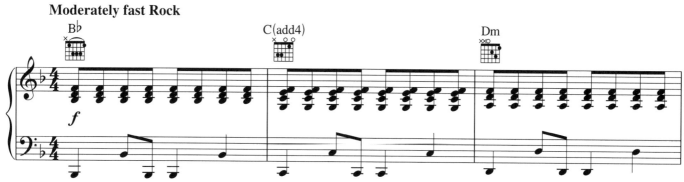

Won - der - ful, so ___

Pow - er - ful, so ___

___ won - der - ful   is   Your   un - fail - ing   love.   Your

___ pow - er - ful,   is   Your   glo - ry   fills   the   sky,   Your

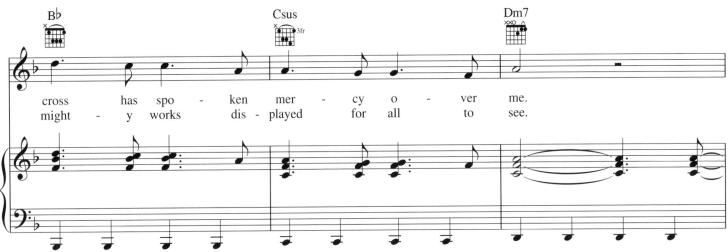

One I love, ___ Beau - ti - ful One I a -

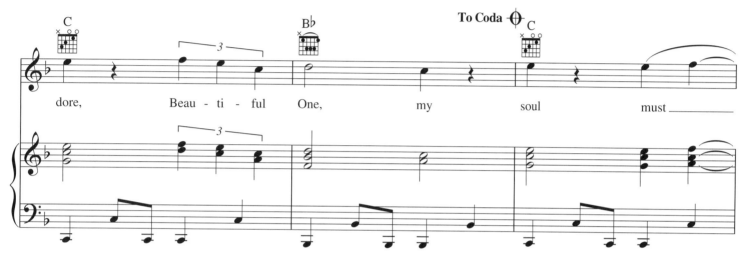

dore, Beau - ti - ful One, my soul must ___

___ sing. ___

Beau - ti - ful

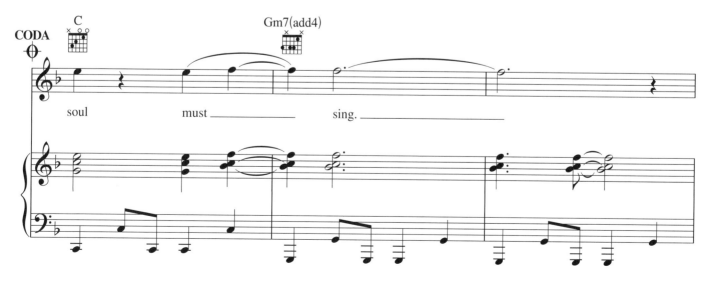

soul must ___ sing. ___

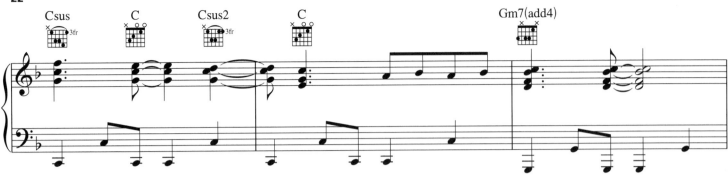

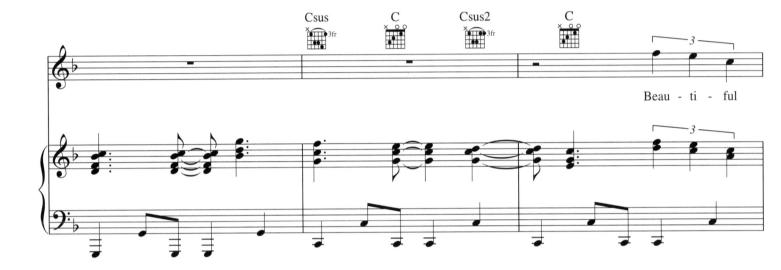

You o - pened my eyes __ to Your won -

- ders a - new, __ You cap - tured my heart with this ___ love, 'cause noth -

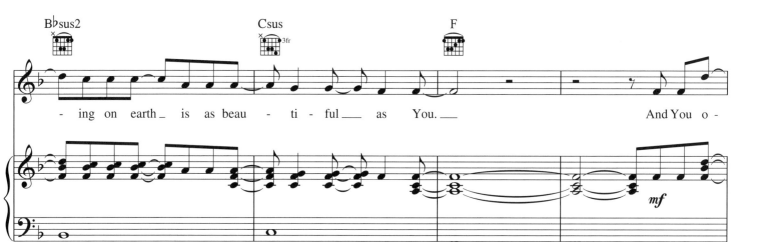

- ing on earth __ is as beau - ti - ful __ as You. __ And You o -

- pened my eyes __ to Your won - ders a - new, __ You cap - tured my heart with this __

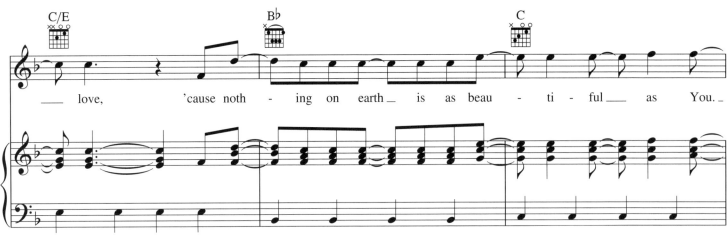

One I love,___ Beau-ti-ful One I a-dore, Beau-ti-ful

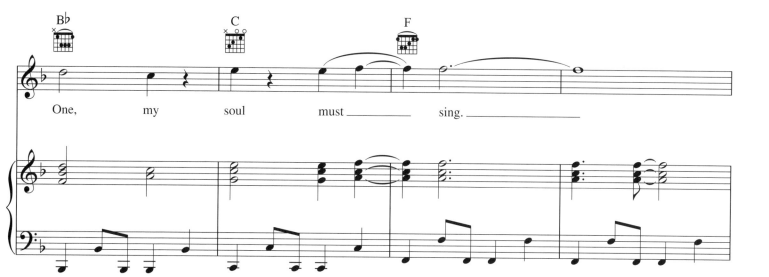

One, my soul must ___ sing. ___

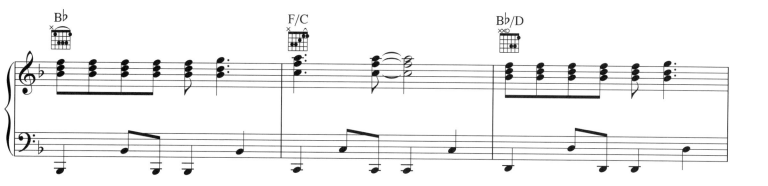

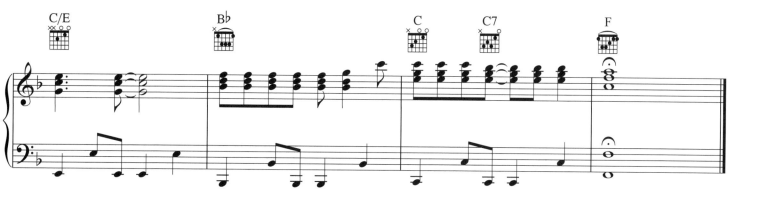

CHRIST IS RISEN

Words and Music by MIA FIELDES
and MATT MAHER

Let no one caught in sin re - main in - side the lie of in - ward shame. We fix our eyes up - on

* Recorded a half step lower.

the cross, _ and run _ to Him _ who showed _ great love _ and bled _

_ for _ us. _ Free - ly You've bled _ for _ us. _

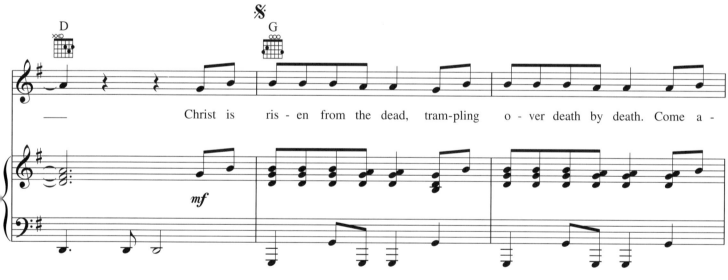

_ Christ is ris - en from the dead, tram-pling o - ver death by death. Come a -

wake, come a - wake, come and rise up from the grave. Christ is ris - en from the dead; we are

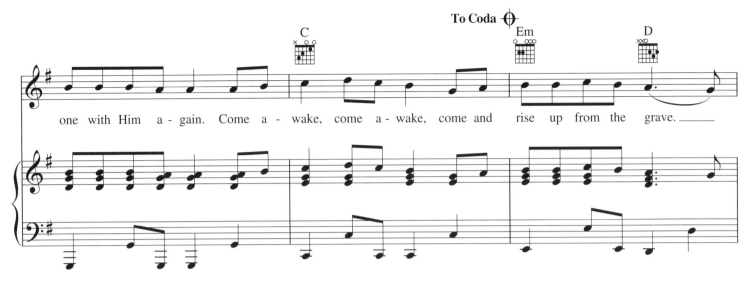

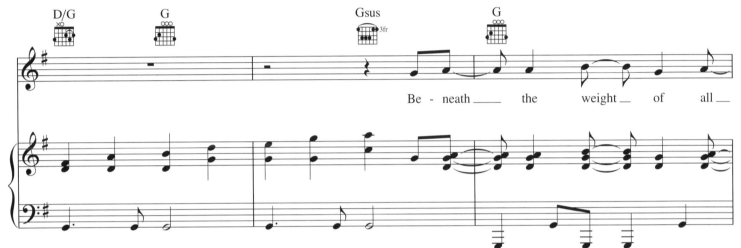

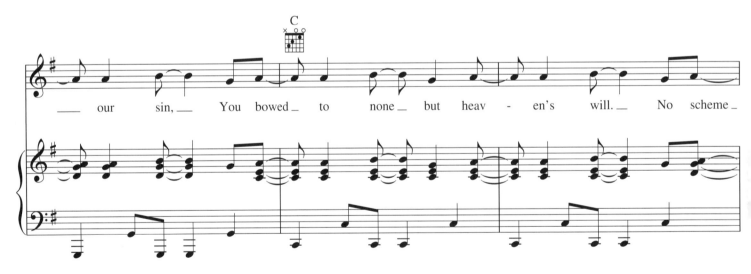

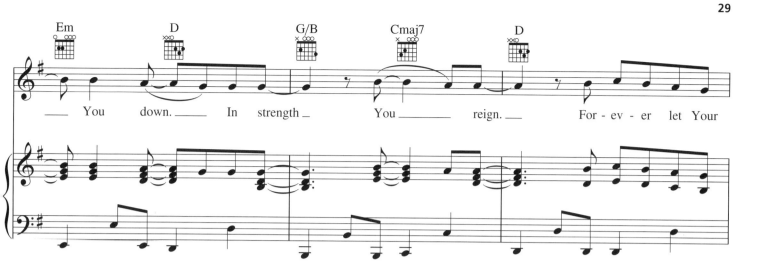

You down. ____ In strength ____ You ____ reign. ____ For - ev - er let Your

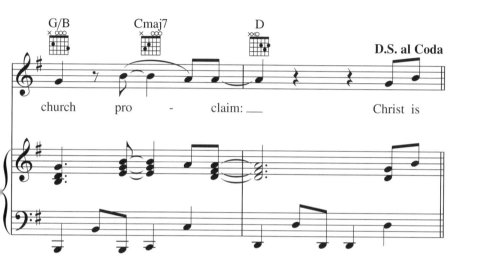

church pro - claim: ____ Christ is

D.S. al Coda

CODA

rise up from the grave.

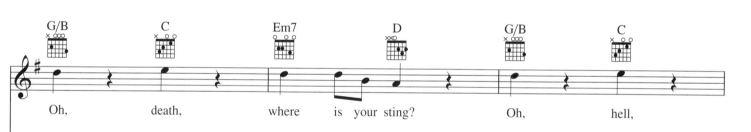

Oh, death, where is your sting? Oh, hell,

where is your vic - to - ry? Oh, church, come

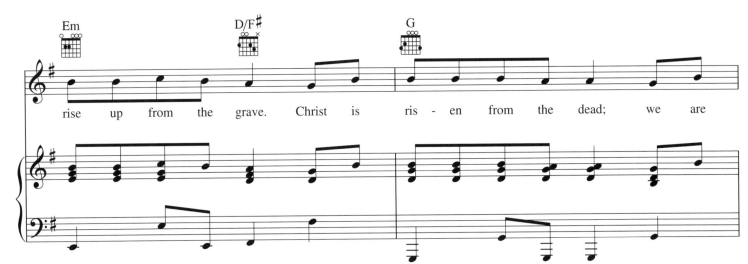

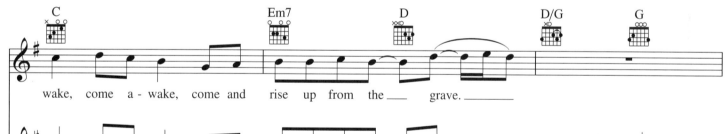

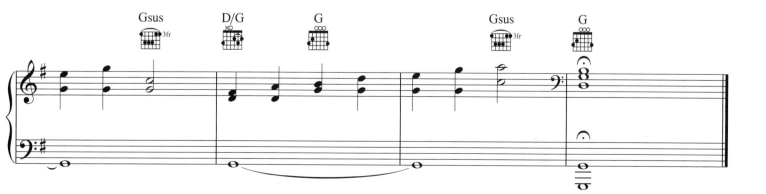

DESERT SONG

Words and Music by
BROOKE FRASER

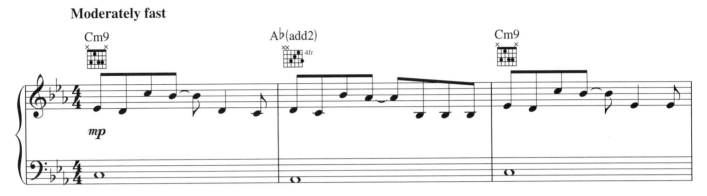

This is ___ my prayer in ___ the
this is ___ my prayer in ___ the

des - ert, ___ when all that's ___ with - in me ___ feels dry.
fi - re, ___ in weak - ness ___ or tri - al ___ or pain.

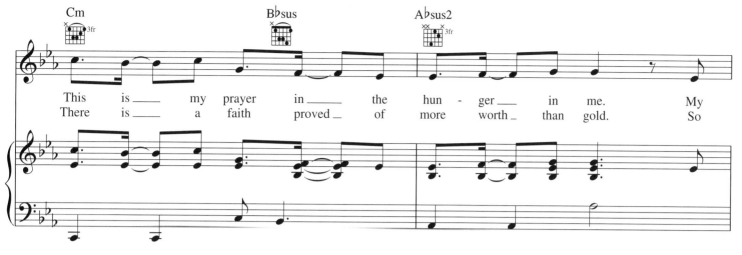

This is ___ my prayer in ___ the hun-ger ___ in me. My
There is ___ a faith proved ___ of more worth ___ than gold. So

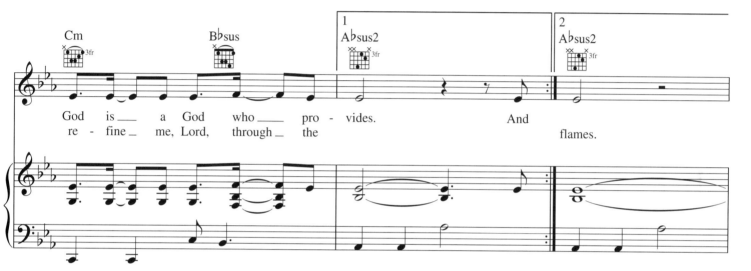

God is ___ a God who ___ pro-vides. And
re-fine ___ me, Lord, through ___ the flames.

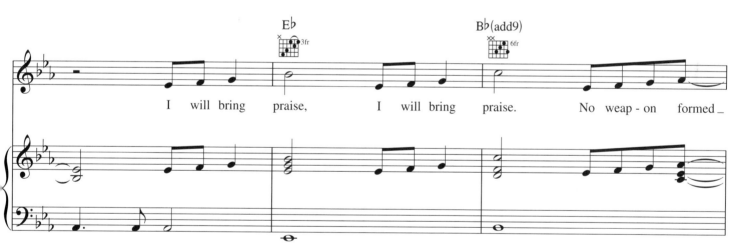

I will bring praise, I will bring praise. No weap-on formed ___

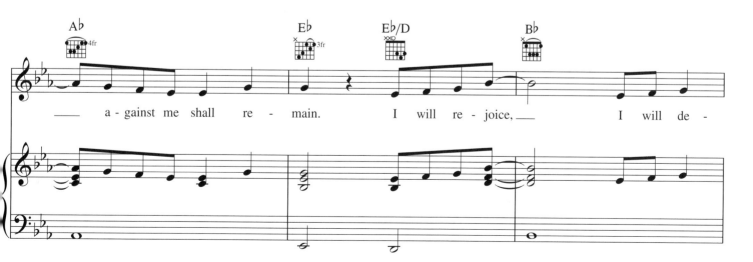

___ a-gainst me shall re-main. I will re-joice, ___ I will de-

34

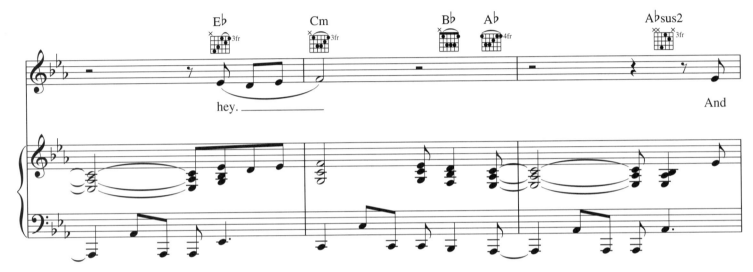

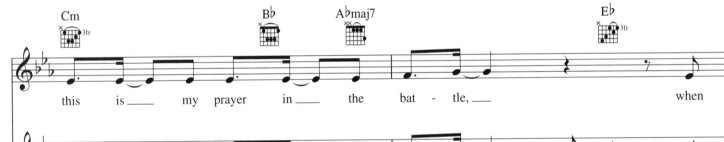

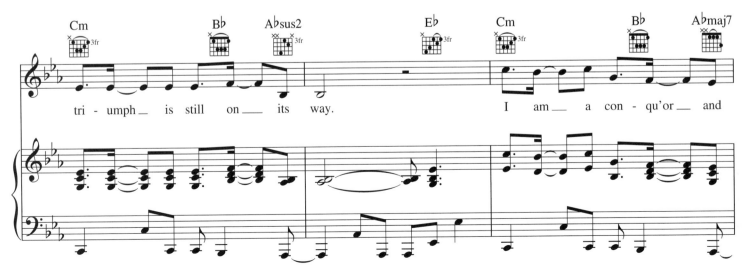

co - heir __ with Christ, so firm on __ His prom - ise __ I'll

stand. I will bring praise, I will bring praise. No weap - on formed __

__ a - gainst me shall re - main. __ I will re - joice, __ I will de -

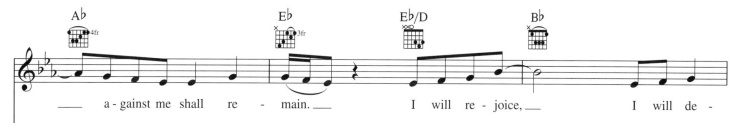

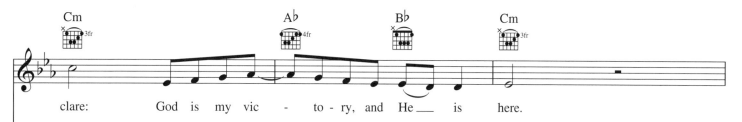

clare: God is my vic - to - ry, and He __ is here.

Oh, _____ all _____ of my life, _____ in _____ ev-'ry sea - son, You _

_____ are still God. __ I _____ have a rea - son to sing. _____ I _

_____ have a rea - son to wor - ship. _____ Yes, __ all _

_____ have a rea - son to wor - ship.

Oh, _____ all _____ of my life, _____ in _____ ev -'ry sea - son, You _____

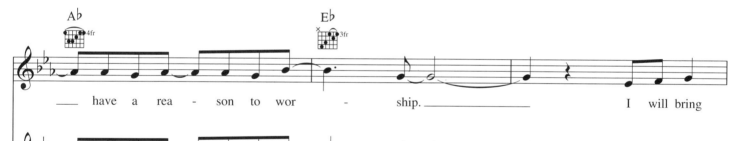

_____ are still God. _____ I _____ have a rea - son to sing. _____ I _____

_____ have a rea - son to wor - ship. _____ I will bring

praise, I will bring praise. No weap - on formed _____ a - gainst me shall re -

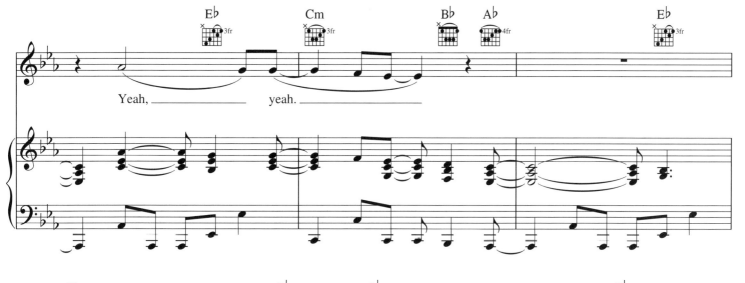

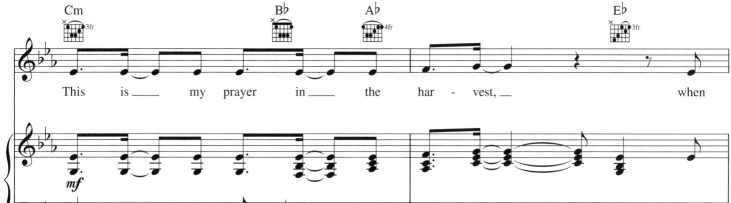

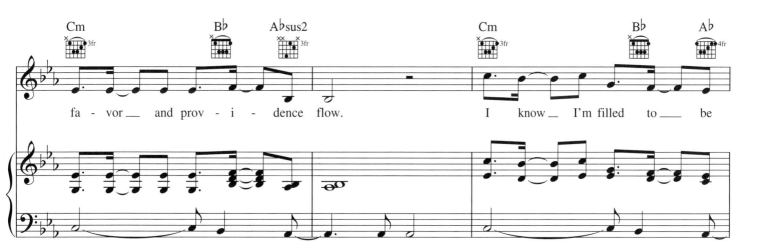

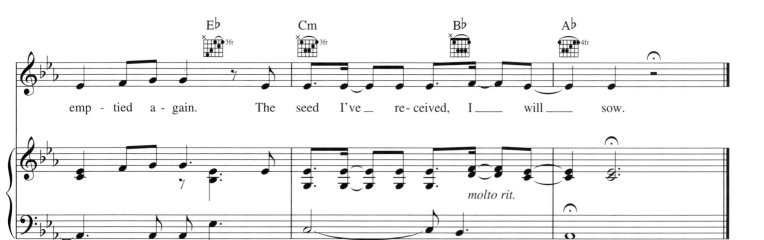

GLORY TO GOD FOREVER

Words and Music by STEVE FEE
and VICKY BEECHING

* Recorded a half step lower.

en - throned a - bove all ___ things. An - gels and saints cry ___ out;
a blaz - ing of - fer - ing, a life that shouts and ___ sings

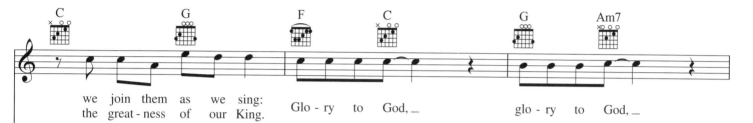

we join them as we sing: Glo - ry to God, __ glo - ry to God, __
the great - ness of our King.

glo - ry to God __ for - ev - er. ___ Glo - ry to God, __

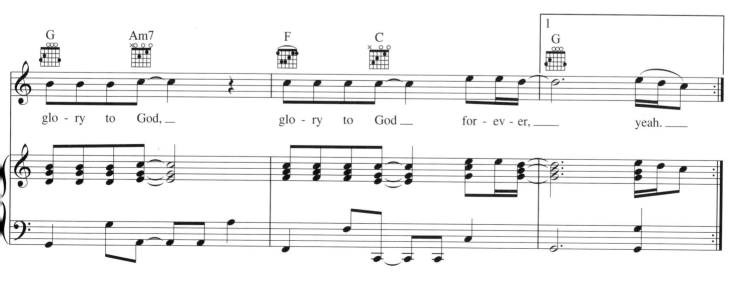

glo - ry to God, __ glo - ry to God __ for - ev - er, ___ yeah. ___

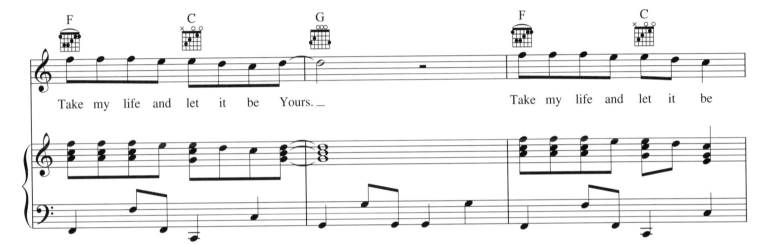

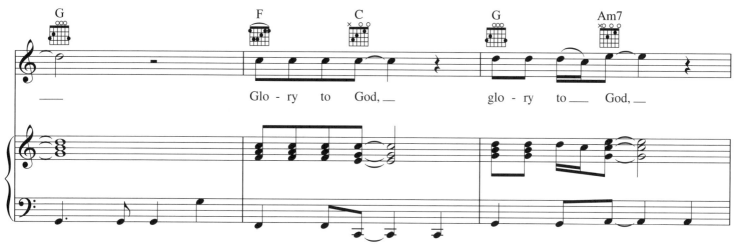

Glo - ry to God, __ glo - ry to __ God, __

glo - ry to God __ for - ev - er. ___ We sing: Glo - ry to God, __

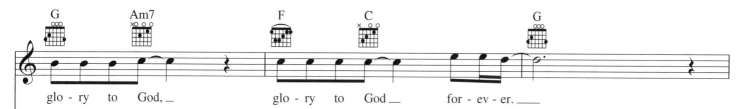

glo - ry to God, __ glo - ry to God __ for - ev - er. ___

Glo - ry to God, __ glo - ry to God, __ glo - ry to God __ for - ev - er. __

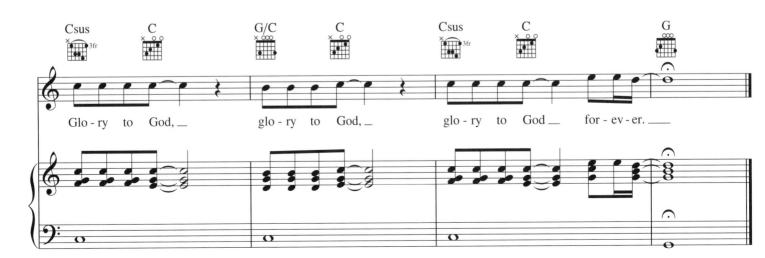

GIVE US CLEAN HANDS

Words and Music by
CHARLIE HALL

dols. So give us clean hands ___ and give us pure ___ hearts. ___

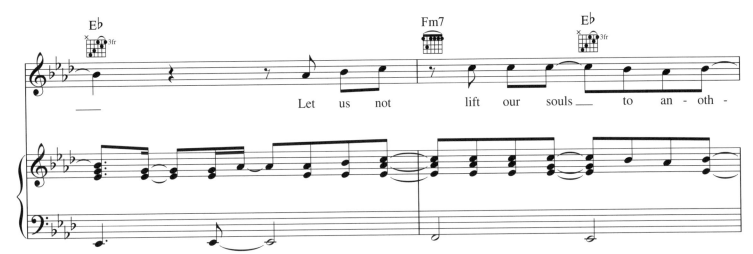

___ Let us not lift our souls ___ to an - oth -

- er. And give us clean hands ___ and give us pure ___ hearts. ___

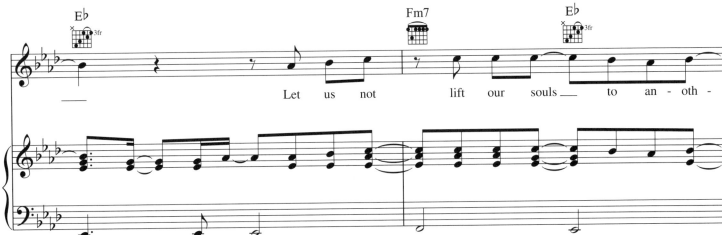

___ Let us not lift our souls ___ to an - oth -

-er. Oh God, let us be a gen-er-a-tion that seeks, _

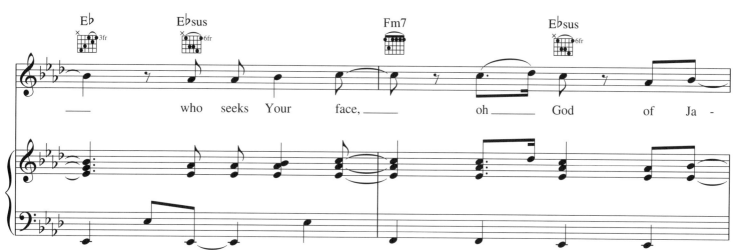

____ who seeks Your face, _____ oh _____ God of Ja -

-cob. Oh God, let us be a gen-er-a-tion that seeks, _

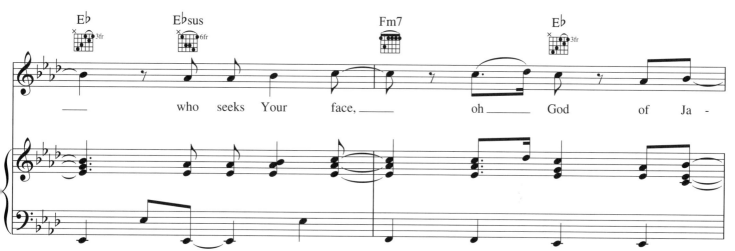

____ who seeks Your face, _____ oh _____ God of Ja -

- cob. —

Oh God of Ja - cob. *Guitar solo ad lib.*

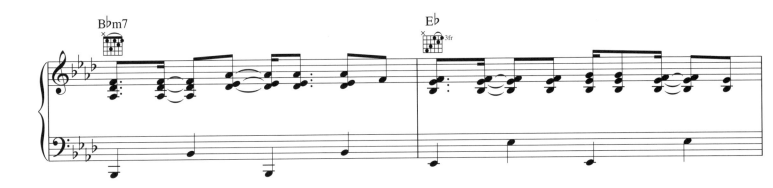

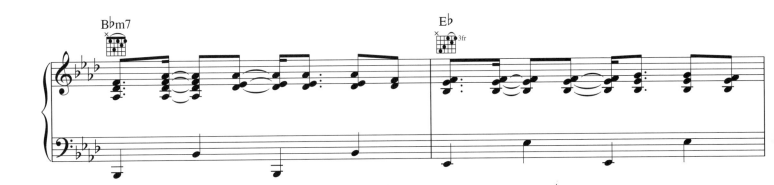

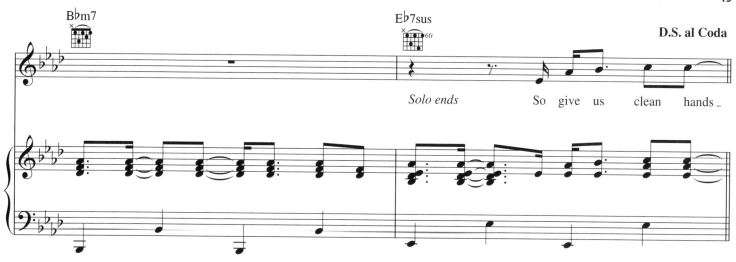

D.S. al Coda

Solo ends   So give us clean hands

CODA

Oh ___ God of Ja - cob. ___

Oh ___ God of Ja - cob. ___

GOD OF THIS CITY

Words and Music by AARON BOYD,
PETER COMFORT, RICHARD BLEAKLEY,
PETER KERNAGHAN, ANDREW McCANN
and IAN JORDAN

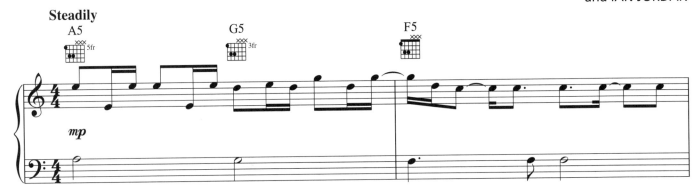

Great - er things have yet to come, and great - er things are still to be done in this __

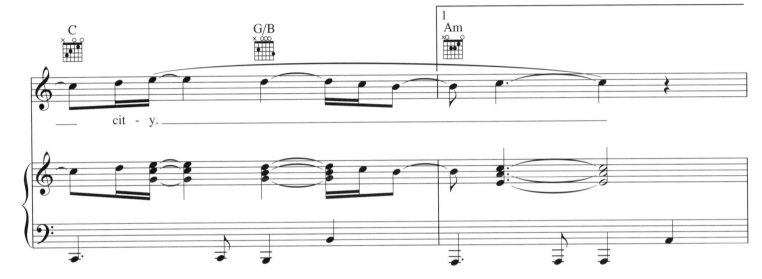

__ cit - y. _____

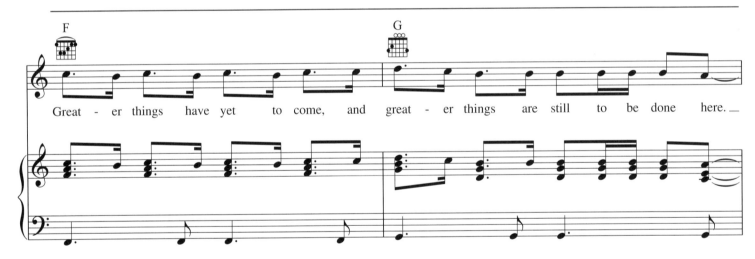

Great - er things have yet to come, and great - er things are still to be done here. __

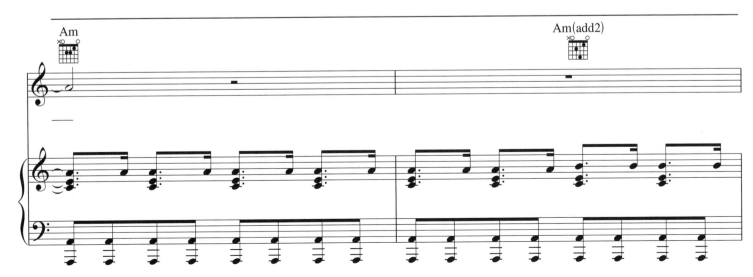

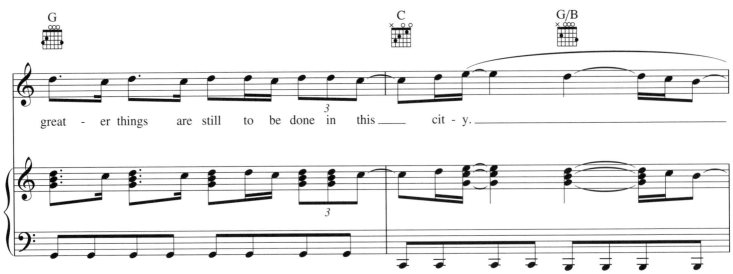

great - er things are still to be done in this ___ cit - y. ___

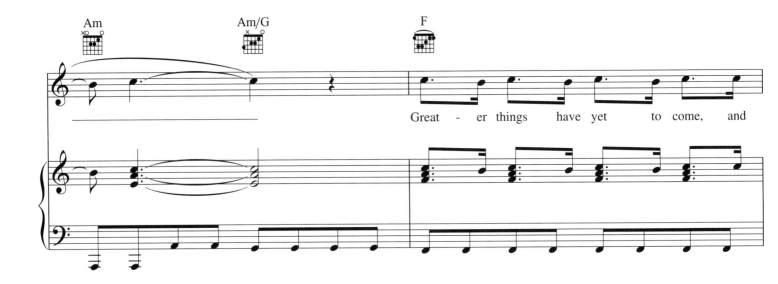

___ Great - er things have yet to come, and

great - er things are still to be done here. __

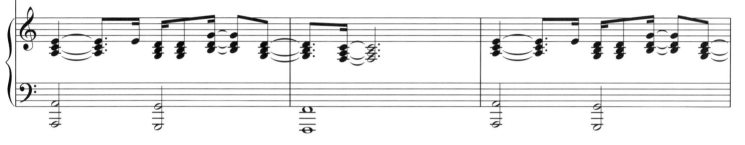

There is no one like __ our ____ God. __ There is no one like __ our __

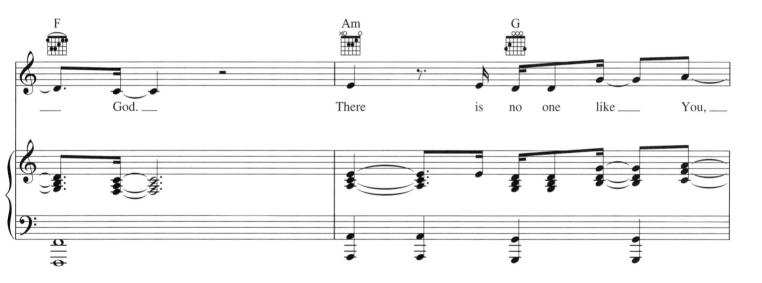

__ God. ___ There is no one like ___ You, __

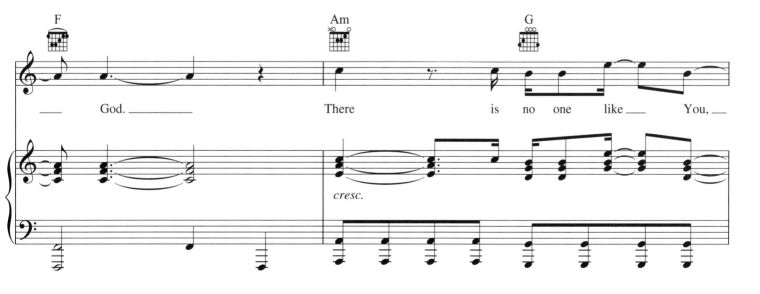

__ God. _____ There is no one like ___ You, __

cresc.

God.

Great - er things have yet to come, and great - er things are still to be done in this _

_ cit - y. _____ Where

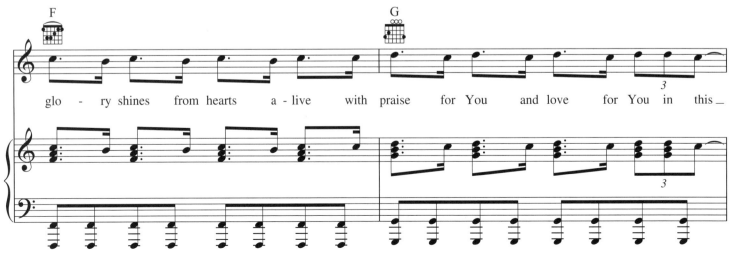

glo - ry shines from hearts a - live with praise for You and love for You in this _

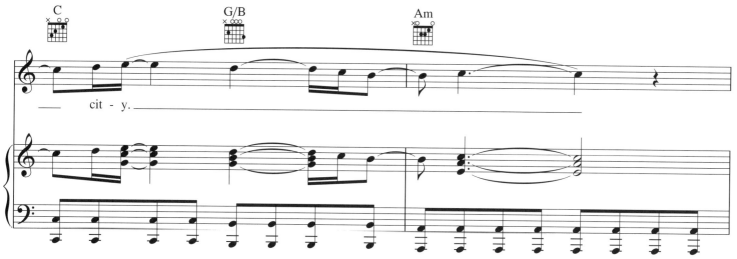

cit - y.

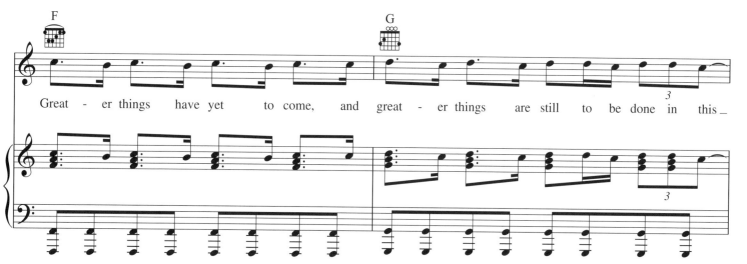

Great - er things have yet to come, and great - er things are still to be done in this ___

cit - y.

Great - er things have yet to come, and great - er things are still to be done here, ___

still ___ to be done ___

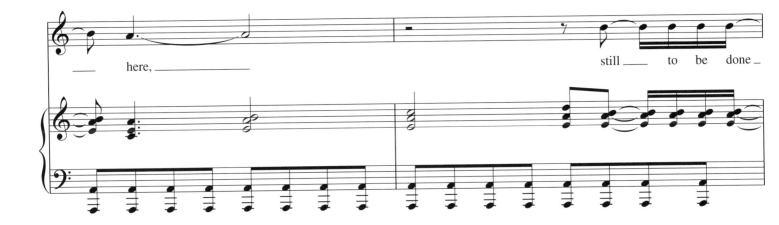

here, _____ still ___ to be done ___

here, _____ still ___ to be done ___

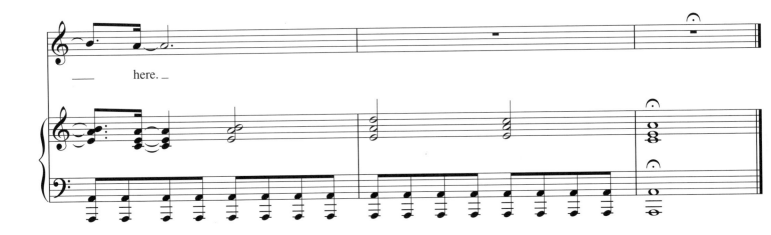

___ here. ___

HAPPY DAY

Words and Music by TIM HUGHES
and BEN CANTELLON

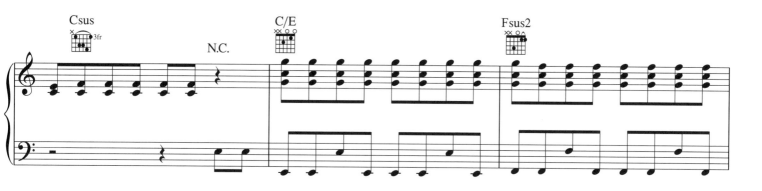

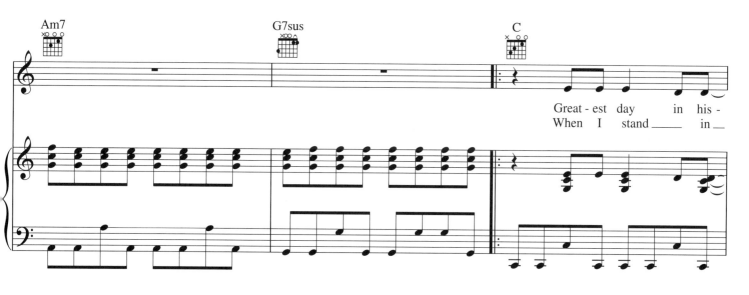

Sing it out, Je-sus is __ a-live. __
I am Yours, Je-sus; You __ are mine. __

Emp-ty cross, the emp-ty grave, __
End-less joy, ___ per-fect peace, __

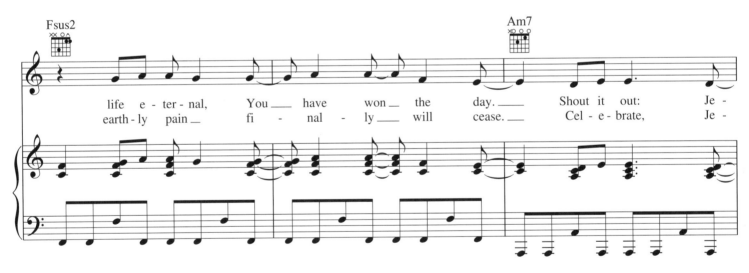

life e-ter-nal, You __ have won __ the day. __ Shout it out: Je-
earth-ly pain __ fi-nal-ly __ will cease. __ Cel-e-brate, Je-

-sus is __ a - live, __ He's a-live. __
-sus is __ a - live, __ He's a-live. __

And oh, _____ hap- py day, _____

_____ hap- py day, _____ You've washed _ my sin a- way.

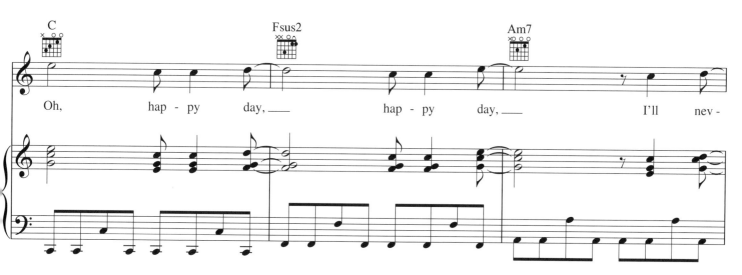

Oh, hap- py day, _____ hap- py day, _____ I'll nev-

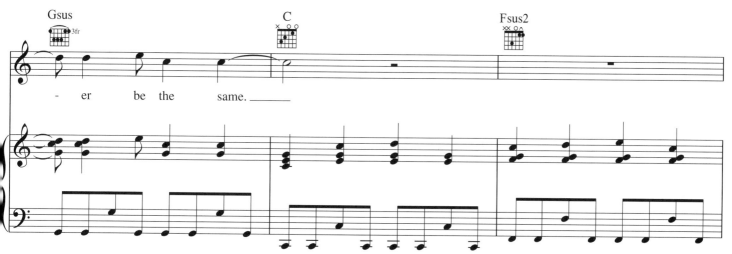

- er be the same. _____

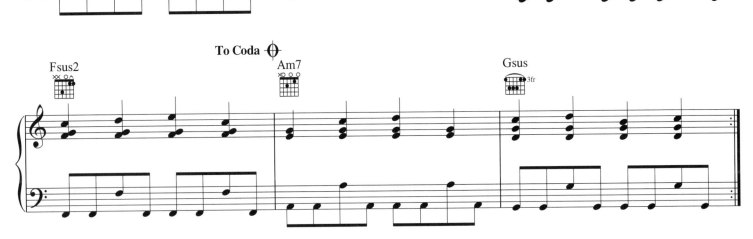

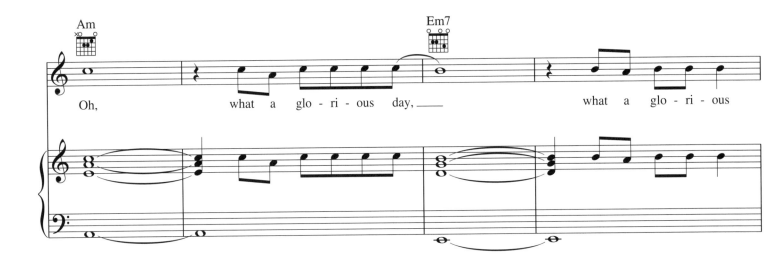

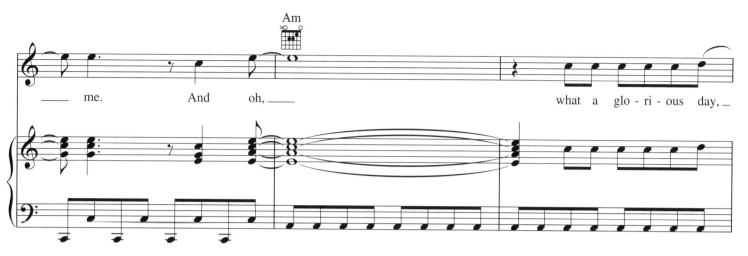

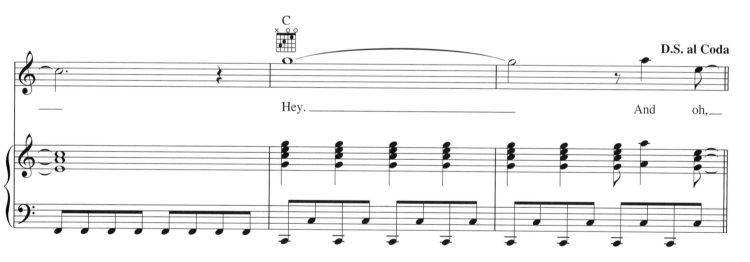

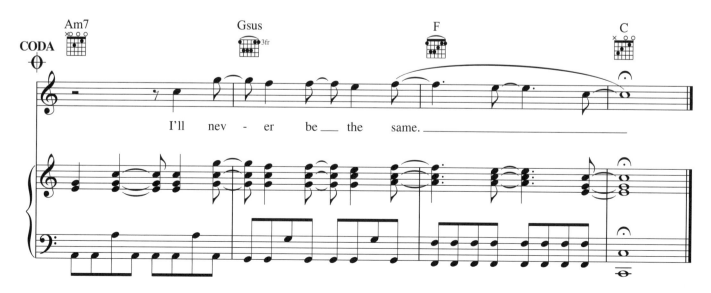

GOD YOU REIGN

Words and Music by LINCOLN BREWSTER
and MIA FIELDES

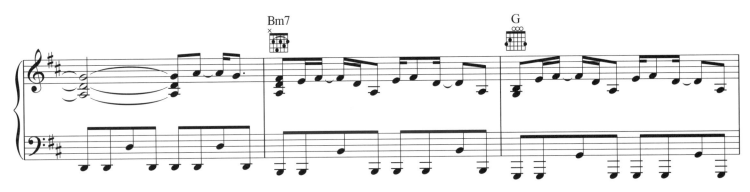

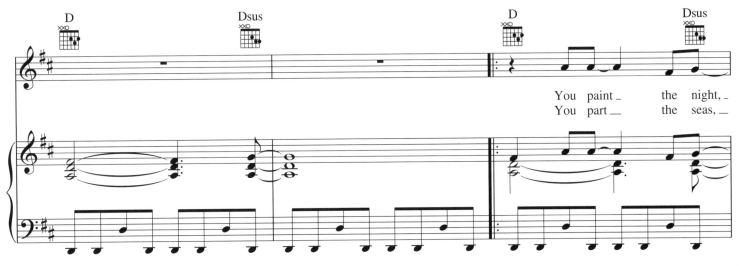

You paint ___ the night, ___
You part ___ the seas, ___

You count ___ the stars ___ and You call them by name.
You move ___ the moun - tains with the words that You say.

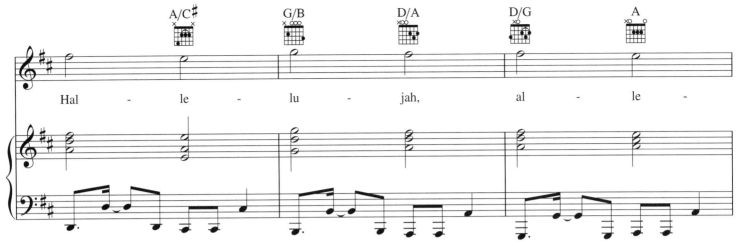

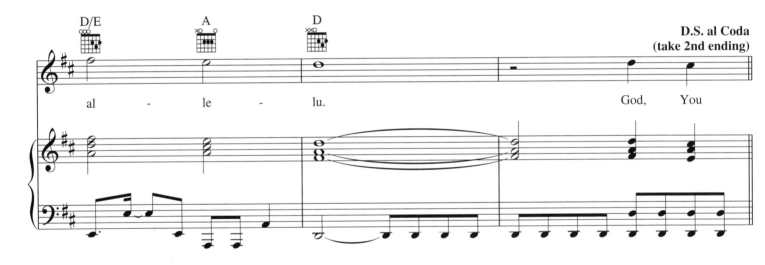

God, You reign.   For - ev - er ___ and

ev - er,   God, You reign.

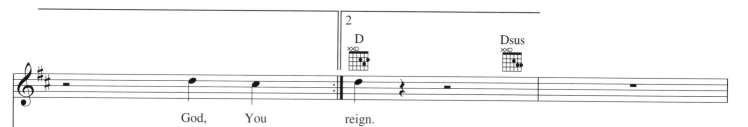

God, You reign.

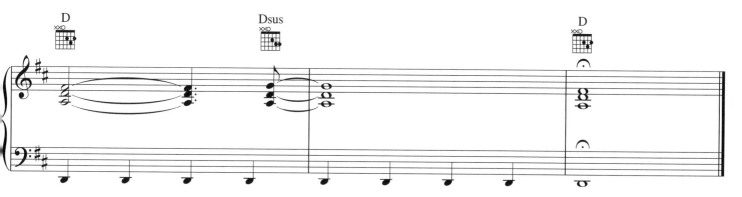

HOW DEEP THE FATHER'S LOVE FOR US

Words and Music by
STUART TOWNEND

deep the Fa-ther's love for us; how vast be-yond all meas-ure that
hold the man up-on a cross, my sin up-on His shoul-ders. A-
will not boast in an-y-thing, no gifts, no pow'r, no wis-dom, but

He should give His on - ly Son to make a wretch His treas - ure. How
shamed, I hear my mock - ing voice call out a - mong the scoff - ers. It
I will boast in Je - sus Christ, His death and res - ur - rec - tion. Why

great the pain of sear - ing loss. The Fa - ther turns His face a - way, as
was my sin that held Him there un - til it was ac - com - plished. His
should I gain from His re - ward? I can - not give an an - swer, but

wounds which mar the Cho - sen One bring man - y sons to glo -
dy - ing breath has brought me life. I know that it is fin -
this I know with all my heart: His wounds have paid my ran -

ry.
ished.

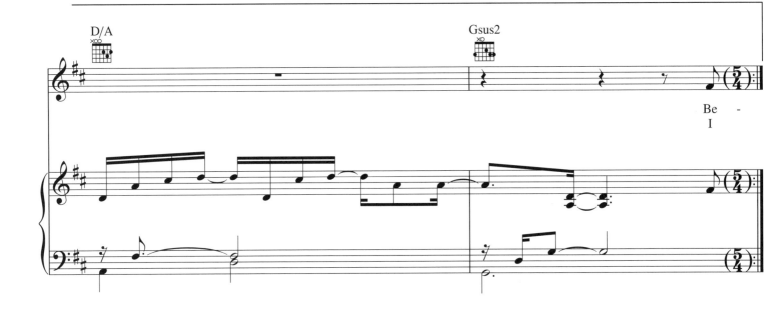

Be -
I

som.   Why should I gain from His re - ward?   I

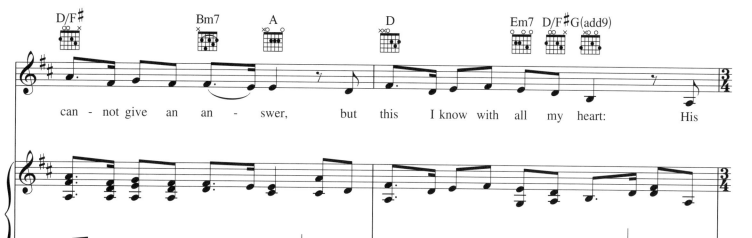

can - not give an an - swer, but this I know with all my heart: His

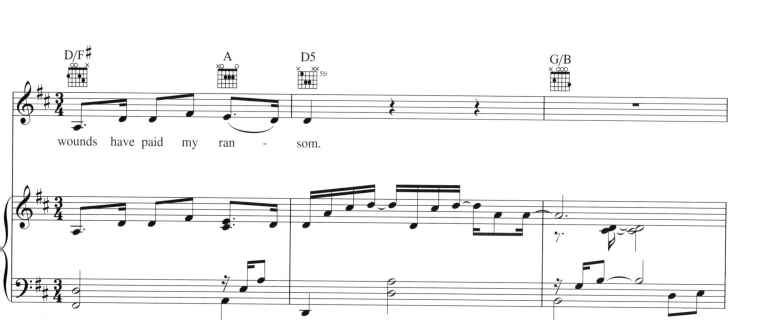

wounds have paid my ran - som.

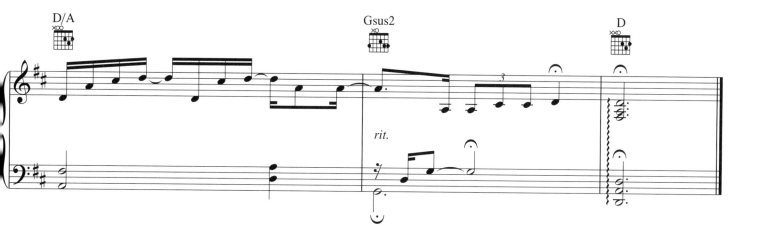

HOW HE LOVES

Words and Music by
JOHN MARK McMILLAN

And all of __ a sud-den, I am un-a-ware of these af-

flic - tions e - clipsed by ___ glo - ry, ___ and I

real - ize ___ just how ___ beau - ti - ful You are, and how

great Your af - fec - tions are ___ for me. ___ And oh,

how He ___ loves us. ___ Oh, oh, how He ___

loves ___ us, ___ how He ___ loves us _____ all.

Yeah, He

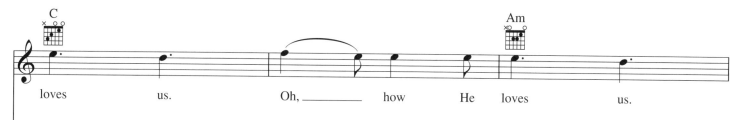

loves   us.   Oh, _____ how   He   loves   us.

Oh, _____ how   He   loves   us.   Oh, _____ how   He

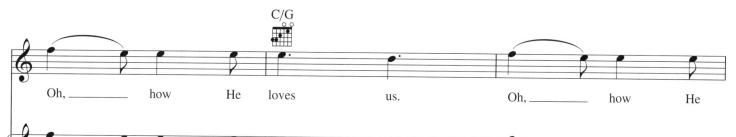

loves. _____ And   we are His __ por - tion and

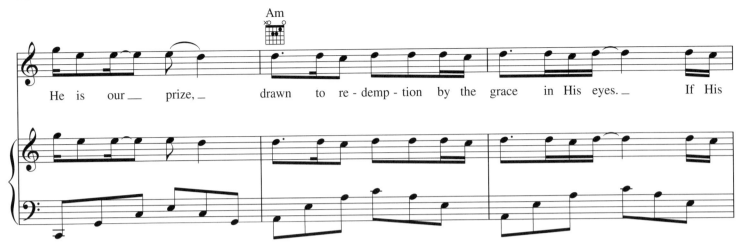

He is our __ prize, __ drawn to re-demp-tion by the grace in His eyes. __ If His

grace is an __ o - cean, __ we're all __ sink - ing. __

And heav-en meets __ earth like an un-fore-seen kiss, and my

heart turns __ vio-lent-ly in-side of my chest. I don't have __ time to main-

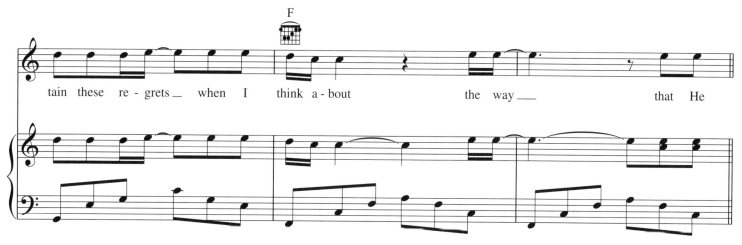

-tain these re-grets __ when I think a-bout the way __ that He

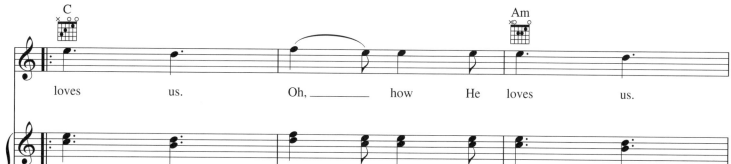

loves us. Oh, __ how He loves us.

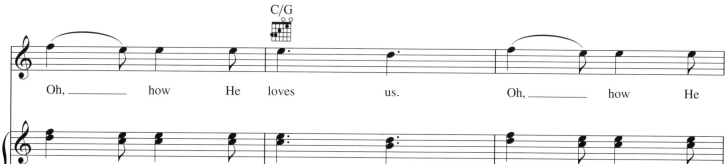

Oh, __ how He loves us. Oh, __ how He

loves. __ Yeah, He __

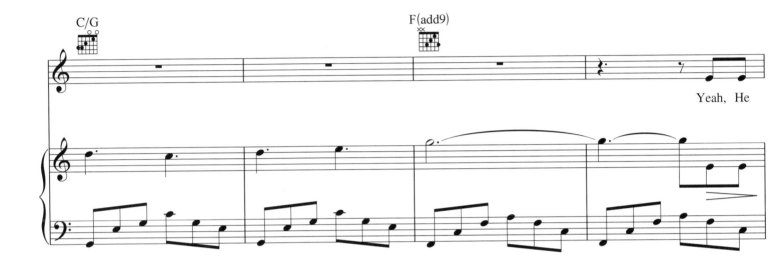

Yeah, He

loves us. Oh, _____ how He loves us. Oh, _____ how He

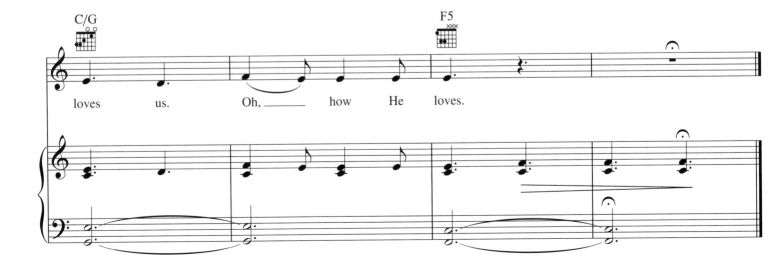

loves us. Oh, _____ how He loves.

MAJESTIC

Words and Music by
LINCOLN BREWSTER

Lord our Lord, how ma-jes-tic is Your name in all the earth.

The heav-ens de-clare Your great-ness, the o-ceans cry

out to You. The moun-tains, they bow down be-fore

You. So I'll join with the earth and I'll give my praise to You.

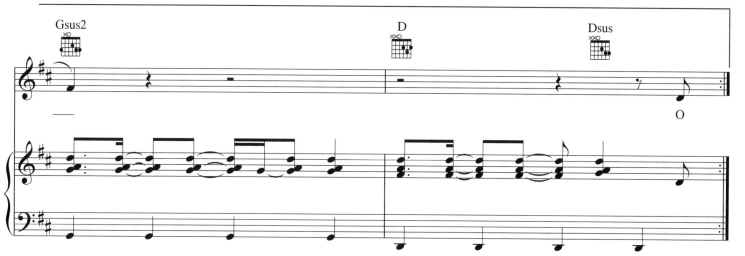

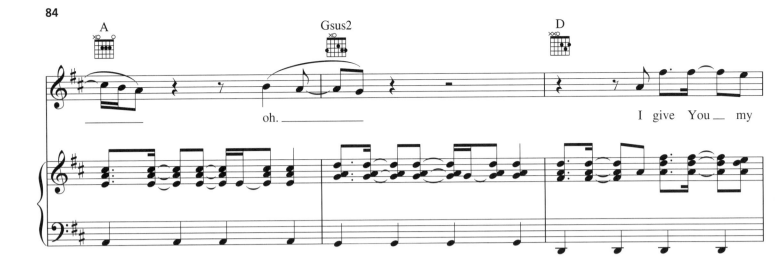

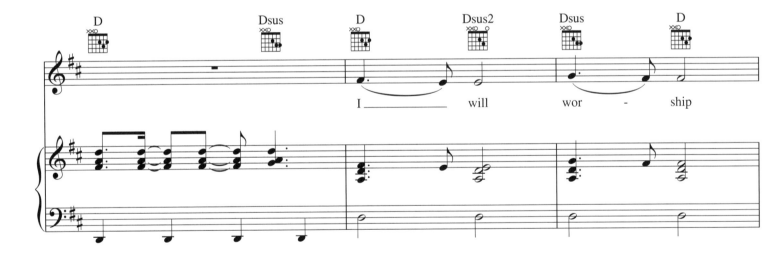

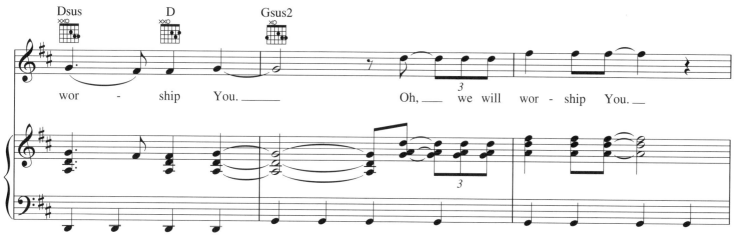

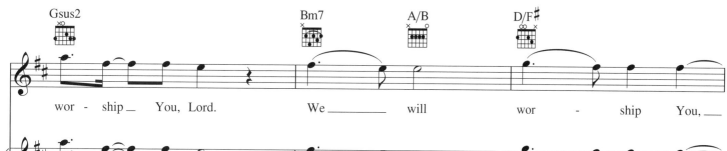

-ness, the o-ceans__ cry out to _____ You. __ The moun-tains, __ they

bow down__ be-fore ____ You. So I'll join ____ with the earth and I'll sing.__

1
Em7   D/F#

_____ The heav-ens __ de - ___ with the earth and I'll give __

2
Em7   D/F#

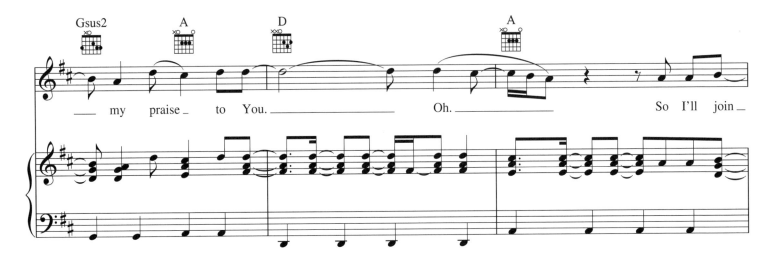

___ my praise__ to You. _____ Oh. _____ So I'll join__

with the earth and I'll give __ my praise _ to You. __ Whoa, _____ whoa. _

_____ So I'll join __ with the earth and I'll give __ my praise _ to You. _

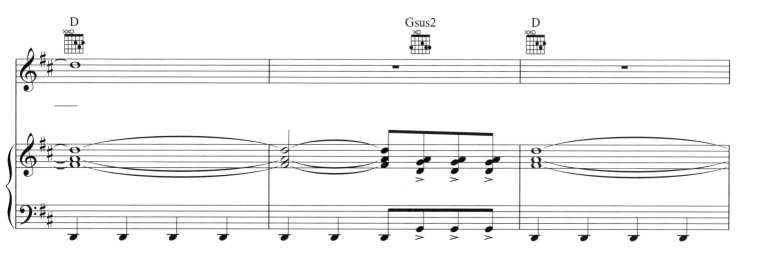

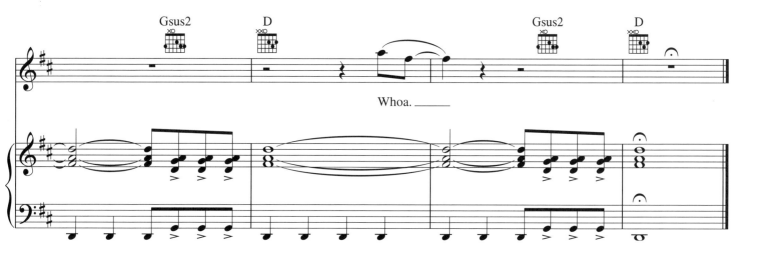

Whoa. _____

INDESCRIBABLE

Words and Music by LAURA STORY
and JESSE REEVES

Joyfully, in two

From the high-est of heights to the depths of the ____
Who has told ev-'ry light-ning bolt where it should ____

____ sea, ____
____ go, ____

cre - a - tion's re -
or seen heav - en - ly

veal - ing Your maj - es - ty.
store - hous - es lad - en with snow?

* *Recorded a half step higher.*

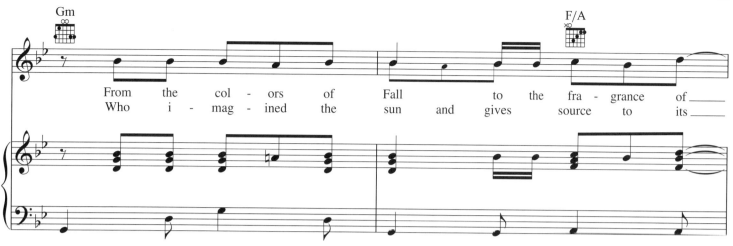

From the col - ors of Fall to the fra - grance of ____
Who i - mag - ined the sun and gives source to its ____

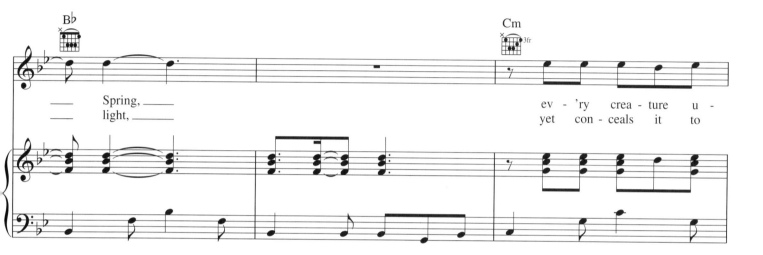

____ Spring, ____ ev - 'ry crea - ture u -
____ light, ____ yet con - ceals it to

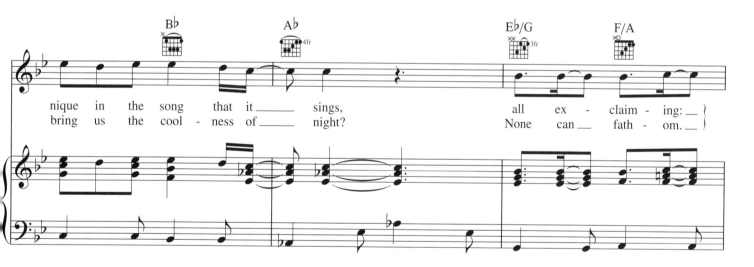

nique in the song that it ____ sings, all ex - claim - ing: ____
bring us the cool - ness of ____ night? None can ____ fath - om. ____

In - de - scrib - a - ble, un - con - tain - a - ble; You placed the stars in the

sky and You know them by ____ name. ____ You are a - maz - ing, ____

____ God. ____ All ___ pow - er - ful,

un - tam - a - ble; awe - struck, we fall to our knees as we hum - bly pro -

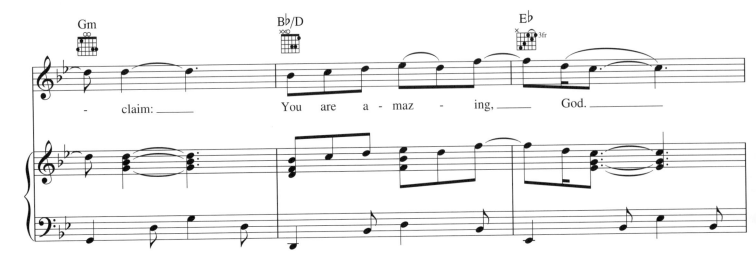

- claim: ____ You are a - maz - ing, ____ God. ____

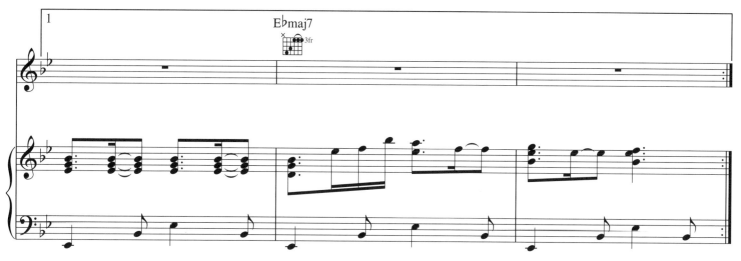

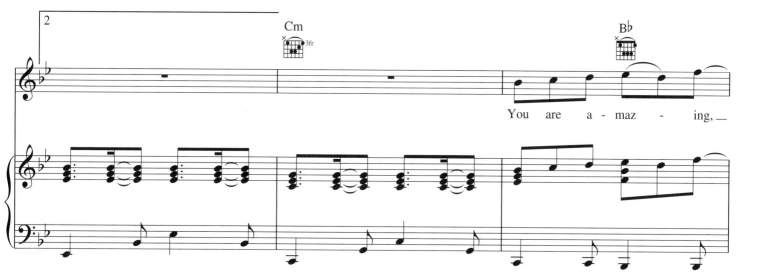

You are a - maz - ing, ___

___ God. _____

In - de - scrib - a - ble, un - con - tain - a - ble; You placed the stars in the

sky and You know them by _____ name. _____ You are a - maz - ing, _

_ God. _____ All _ pow - er - ful,
In - com - p'ra - ble,

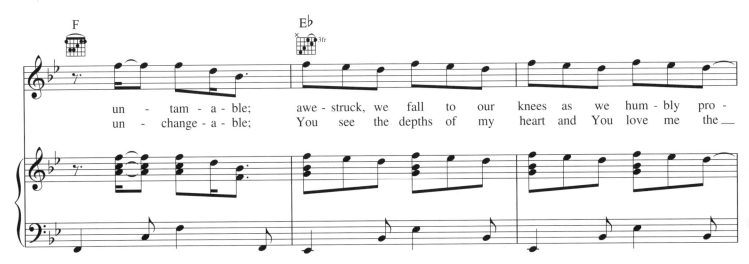

un - tam - a - ble; awe - struck, we fall to our knees as we hum - bly pro -
un - change - a - ble; You see the depths of my heart and You love me the __

Gm   B♭/D   E♭

- claim: _____
___ same; _____   You are a - maz - ing, _____ God. _____

1   2   E♭maj7

You are a - maz - ing, _____ God. _____

rit.

JESUS PAID IT ALL

Words and Music by
ALEX NIFONG

Recorded a half step lower.

Je - sus paid it all, all to Him I owe.

Sin had left a crim-son stain; He washed it white as snow.

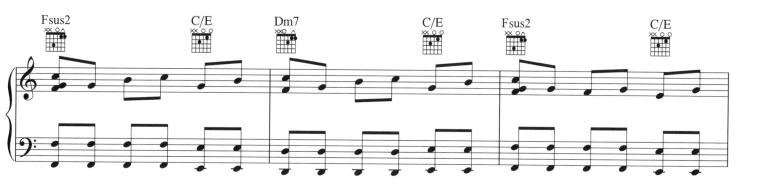

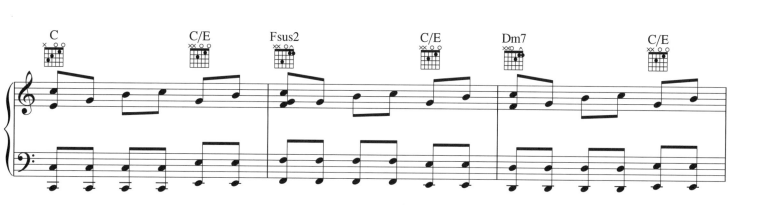

Lord, _ now in - deed I find Thy pow'r, and Thine a -
when be - fore the find throne I stand in Him com -

lone, can _ change the lep - er's spots and _
plete, "Je - sus died, my soul to save," my _

melt the heart of stone. Je - sus paid it all,
lips shall still re -

all to Him I owe. My sin had left this crim - son stain; He

washed it white as snow. It's washed a - way, ___ all ___ my

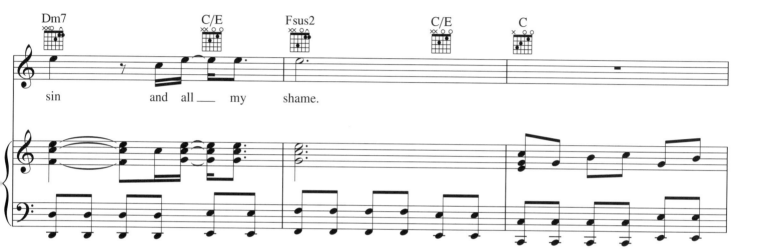

sin and all ___ my shame.

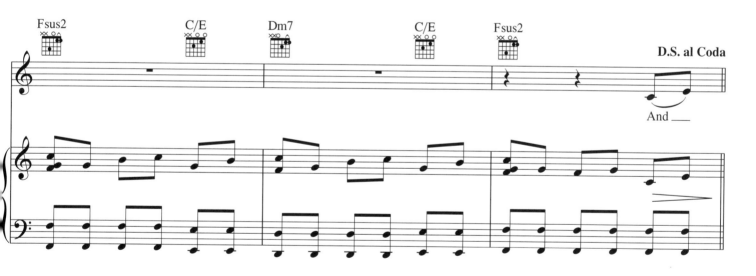

D.S. al Coda

And ___

peat. Je - sus paid it all, all to Him I

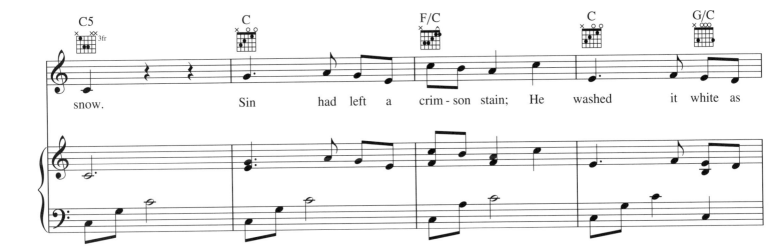

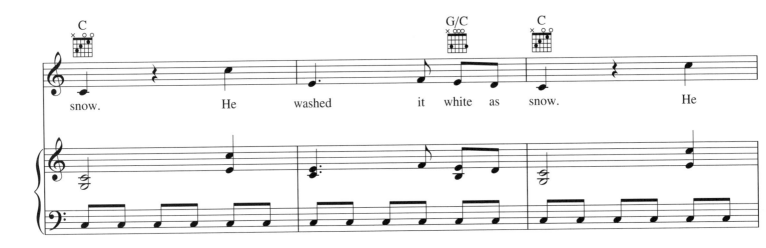

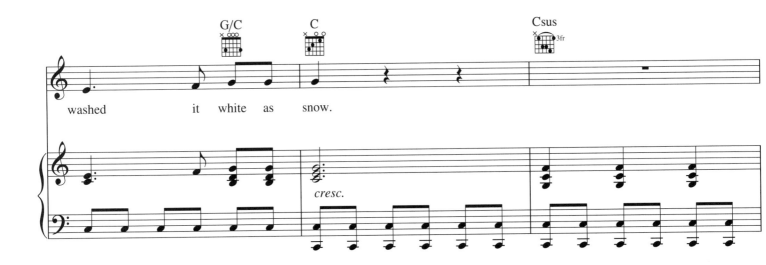

LET GOD ARISE

Words and Music by CHRIS TOMLIN,
JESSE REEVES and ED CASH

With a driving beat

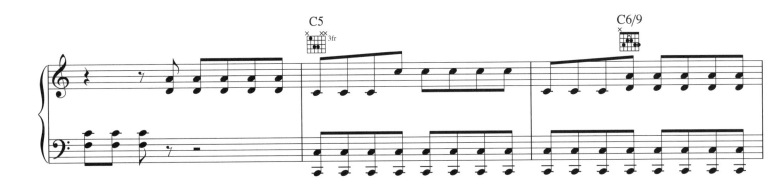

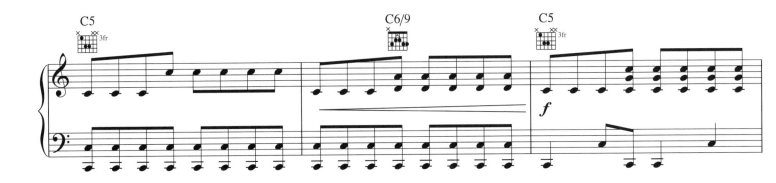

Hear the ho -

* *Recorded a half step lower.*

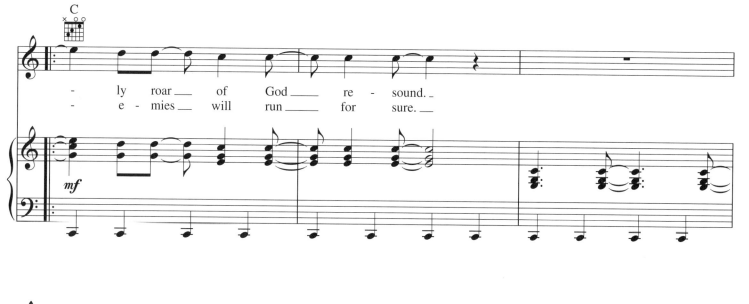

-ly roar ___ of God ___ re - sound. ___
-e - mies ___ will run ___ for sure. ___

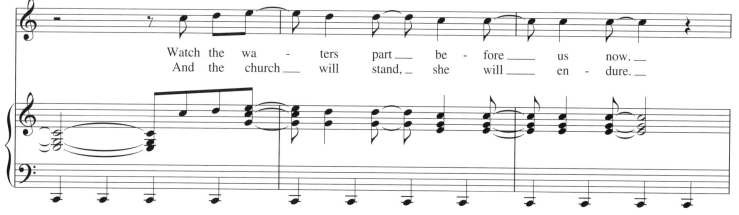

Watch the wa - ters part ___ be - fore ___ us now. ___
And the church ___ will stand, __ she will ___ en - dure. ___

Come and see _____ what He ___ has done _
And He holds ___ the keys ___ of life, __

___ for us. ___ Tell the world _ of His ___ great love. _ Our __ God _
___ our Lord. _ Death has ___ no sting, _ no fi - nal word. _

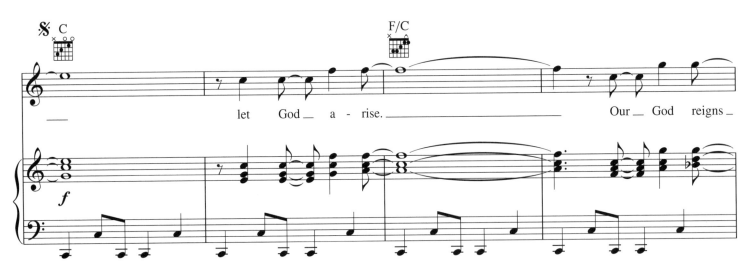

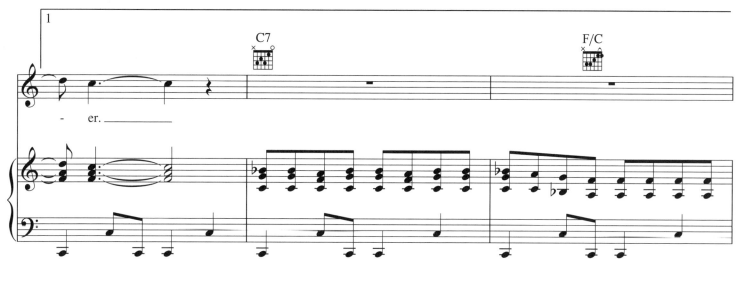

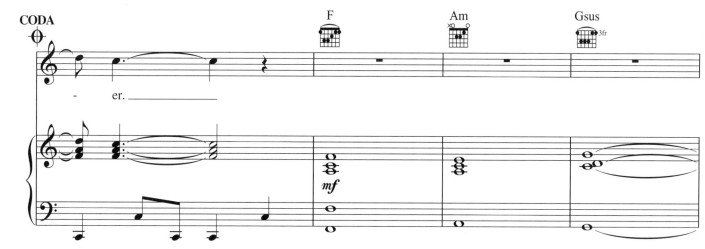

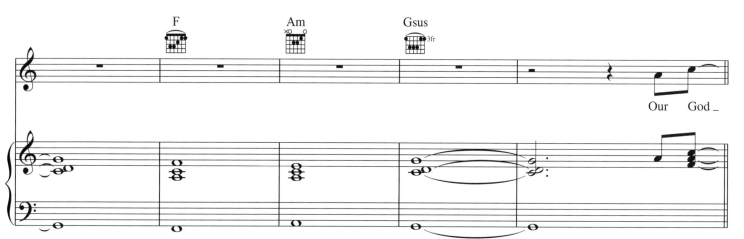

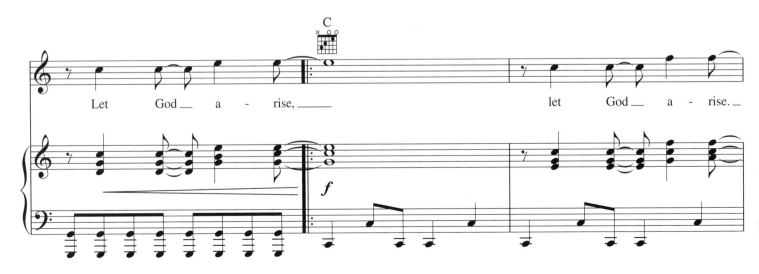

Our __ God reigns __ now and for-ev-

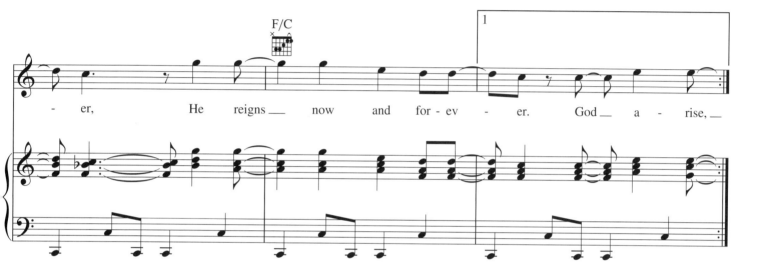

- er, He reigns __ now and for-ev - er. God __ a - rise, __

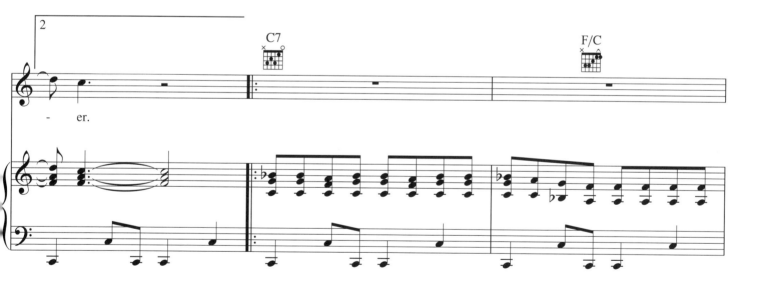

- er.

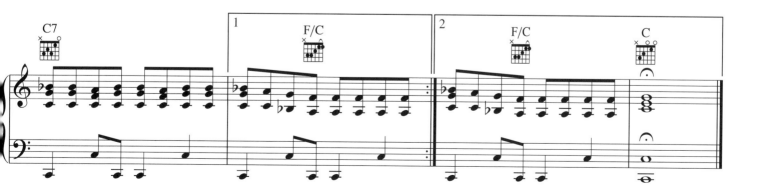

THE LORD REIGNS

Words and Music by
KLAUS KUEHN

With excitement

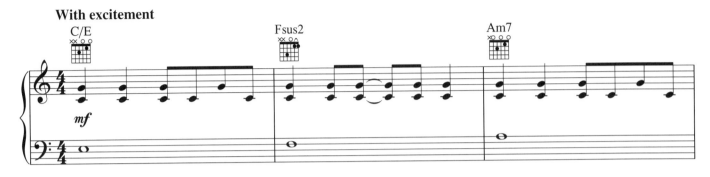

The Lord reigns; let the

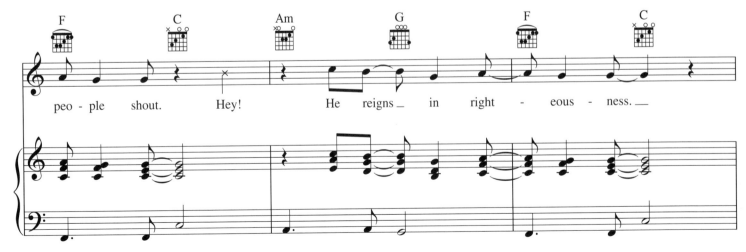

peo - ple shout. Hey! He reigns ___ in right - eous - ness. ___

Let the heav-ens be glad, let the earth re - joice. ___

The Lord reigns; let the peo - ple clap ___ their hands.

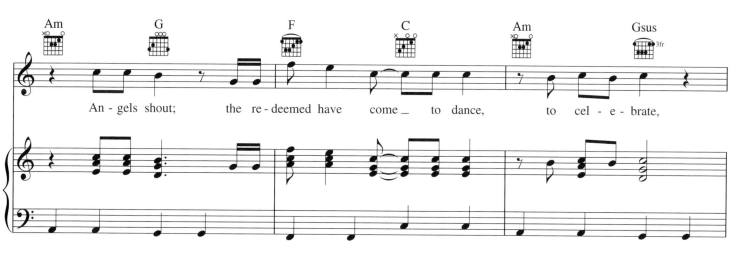

An - gels shout; the re - deemed have come ___ to dance, to cel - e - brate,

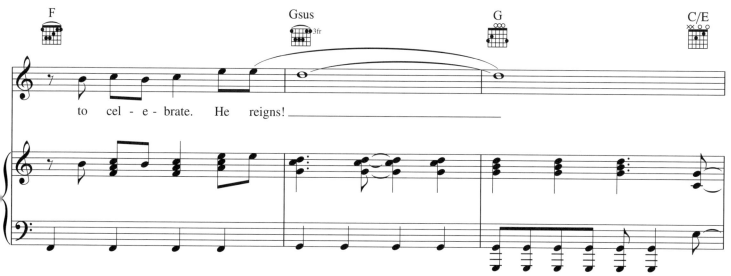

to cel - e - brate. He reigns! _____

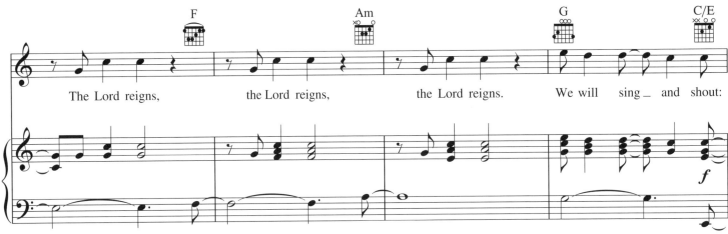

The Lord reigns, the Lord reigns, the Lord reigns. We will sing __ and shout:

You reign, You reign, You reign, for -

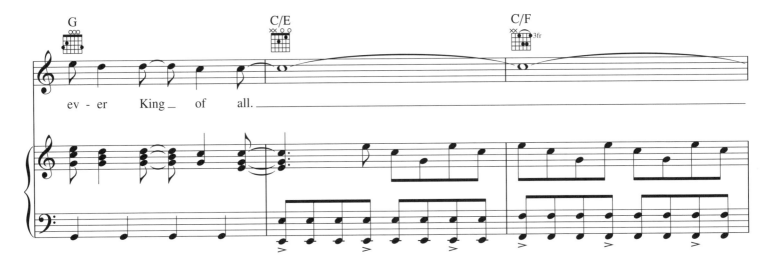

ev - er King __ of all. _____

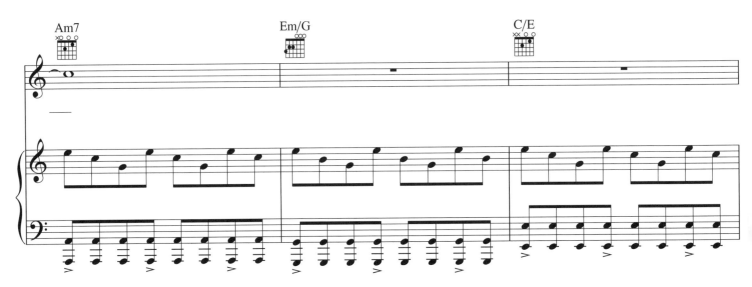

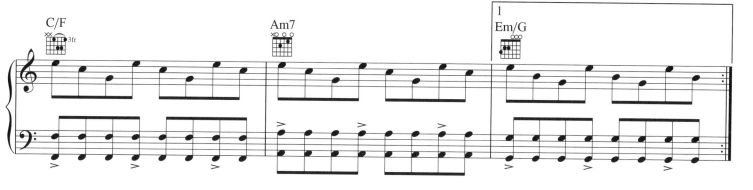

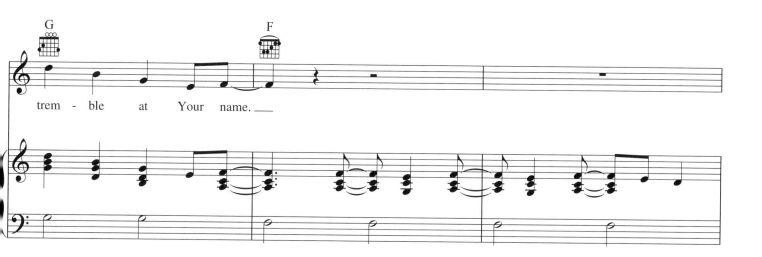

Let all the peo - ple sing of

Your awe - some pow'r in all ___ the earth. Let dark - ness

trem - ble at Your name. ___

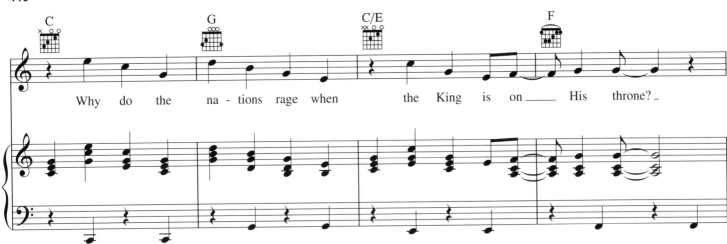

Why do the na - tions rage when the King is on ___ His throne? ___

Now and ___ for - ev - er, You ___ will reign. ___

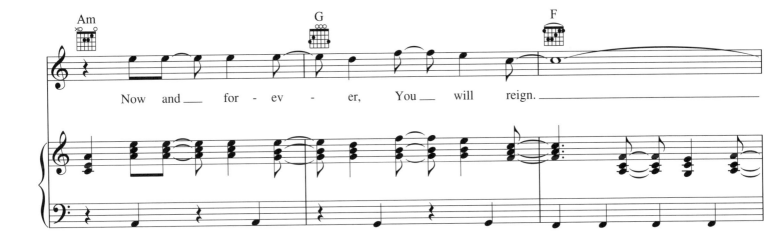

___ Let all the peo - ple sing of

Your awe - some pow'r in all ___ the earth. Let dark - ness

trem - ble at Your name. __

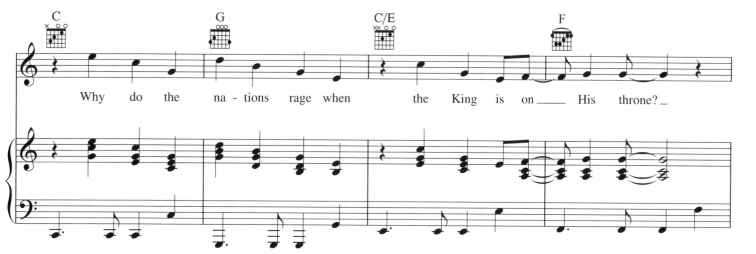

Why do the na - tions rage when the King is on __ His throne? __

Now and __ for - ev - er, You __ will reign. __ Oh! __

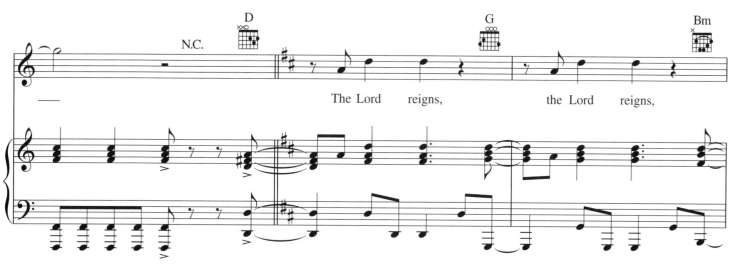

__ The Lord reigns, the Lord reigns,

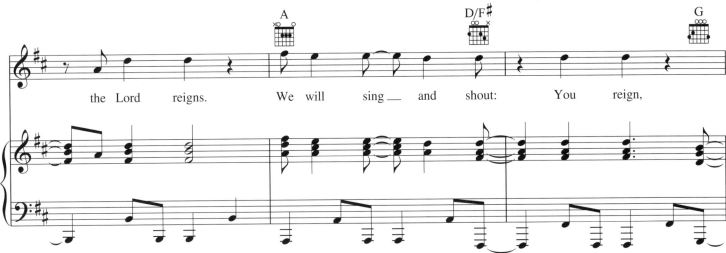

the Lord reigns. We will sing__ and shout: You reign,

You reign, You reign, for- ev- er King__ of all.__

__ The Lord reigns, the Lord reigns, the Lord reigns.

We will sing__ and shout: You reign, You reign,

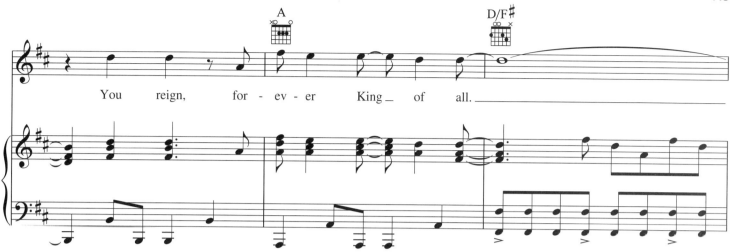

You reign, for - ev - er King _ of all. _____

_____ For - ev - er King _ of all. _

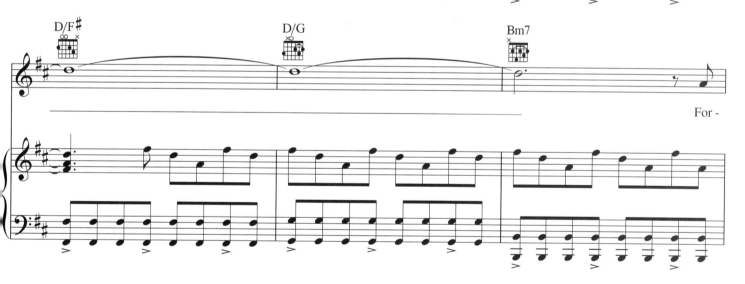

For -

ev - er King _ of all. _____

A NEW HALLELUJAH

Words and Music by PAUL BALOCHE,
MICHAEL W. SMITH and DEBBIE SMITH

reach to the oth - er side.

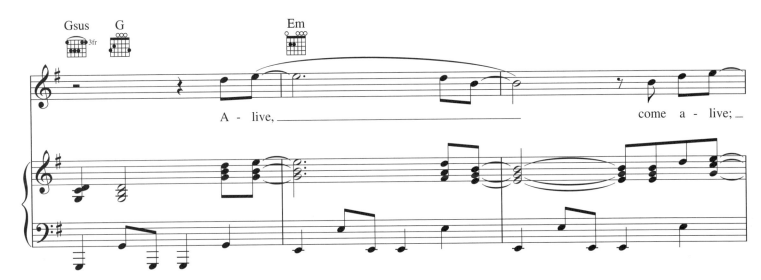

A - live, come a - live;

let the song a - rise.

To Coda ⊕

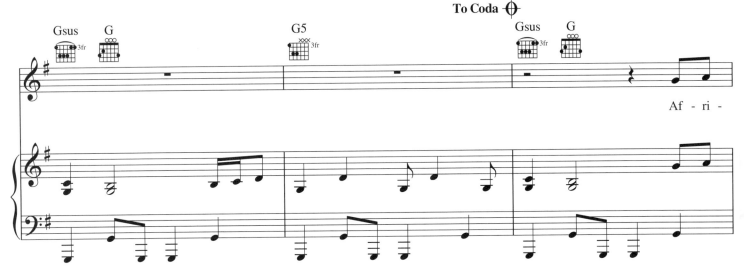

Af - ri -

ca sings a new song, reach-ing out with a new __ hal - le -

lu - jah. Ev - 'ry son and ev - 'ry daugh - ter, ev - 'ry -

one sing a new __ hal - le - lu - jah.

D.S. al Coda

A - rise, __

Let the song a - rise, ___ yeah. ___

Let the song a - rise. ___

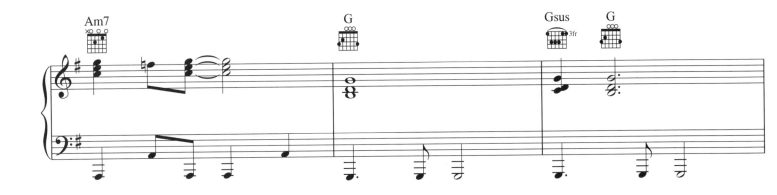

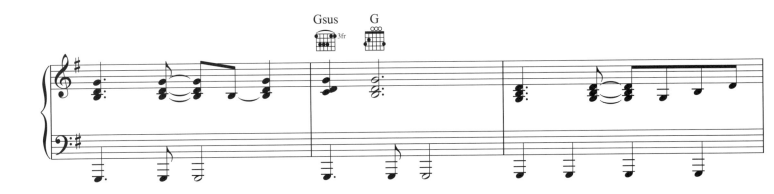

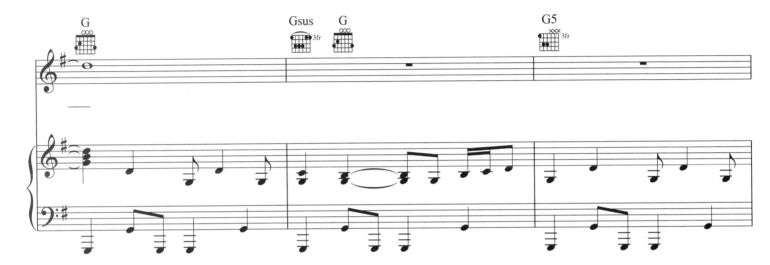

MIGHTY TO SAVE

Words and Music by BEN FIELDING
and REUBEN MORGAN

ev - 'ry - one needs com - pas - sion, a love that's nev - er fail -

take __ me as You find __ me, all my fears and fail -

-ing.
-ures, Well, let mer - cy
and fill my

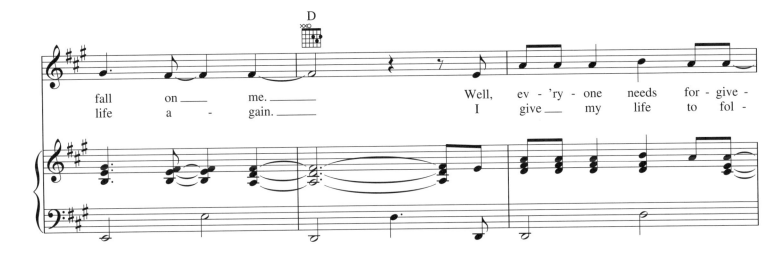

fall on ___ me. ___ Well, ev - 'ry - one needs for - give -
life a - gain. ___ I give ___ my life to fol -

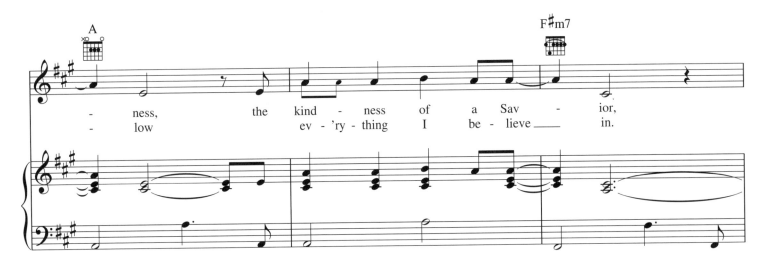

- ness, the kind - ness of a Sav - ior,
- low ev - 'ry - thing I be - lieve ___ in.

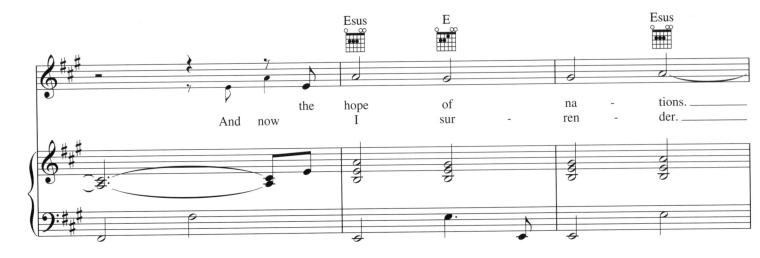

the hope of na - tions. ___
And now I sur - ren - der. ___

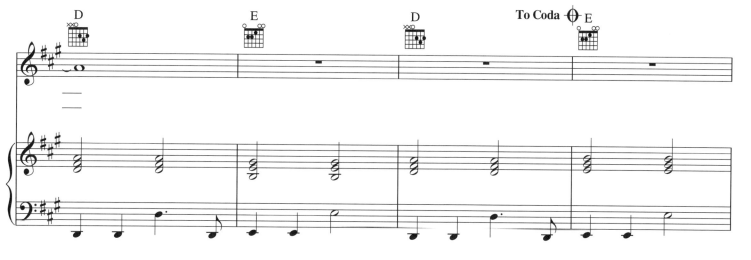

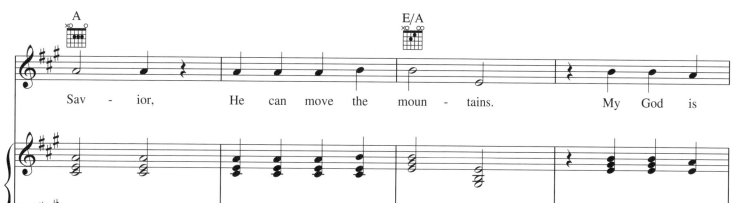

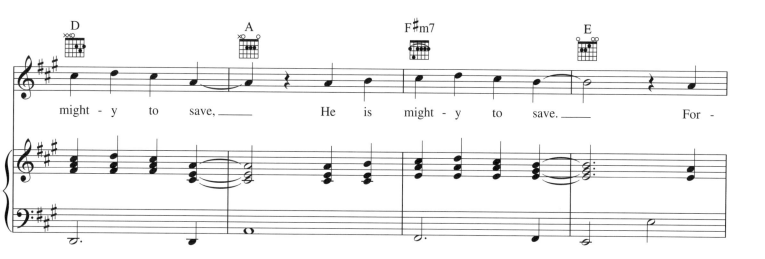

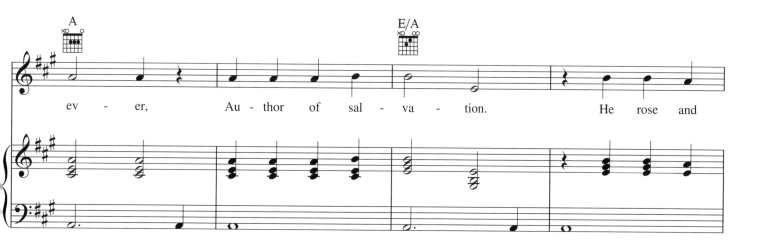

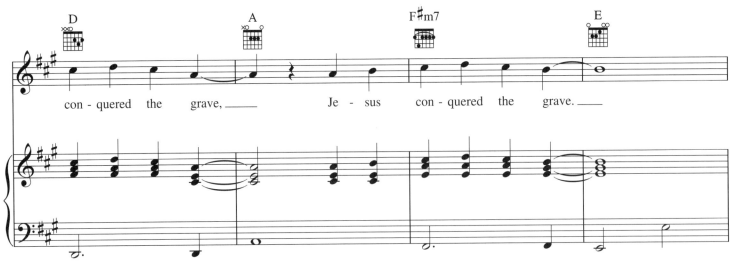

con - quered the grave, _____ Je - sus con - quered the grave. _____

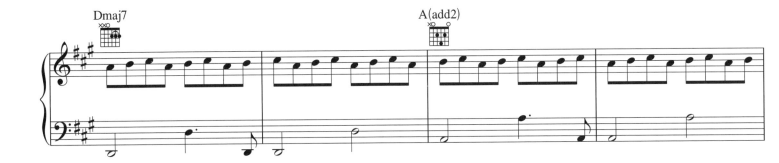

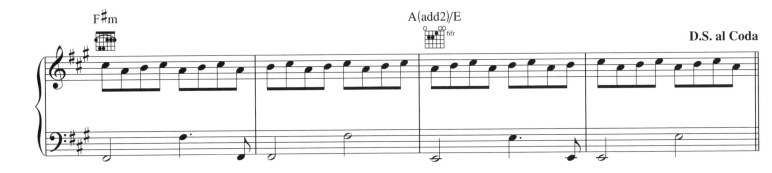

D.S. al Coda

Sav - ior, He can move the

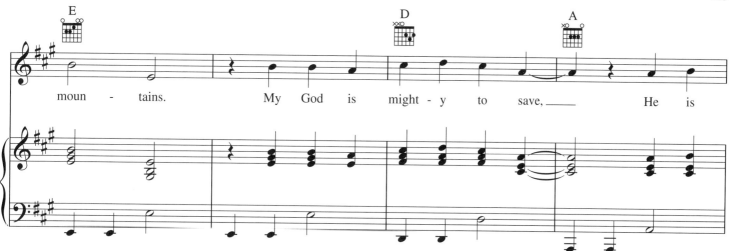

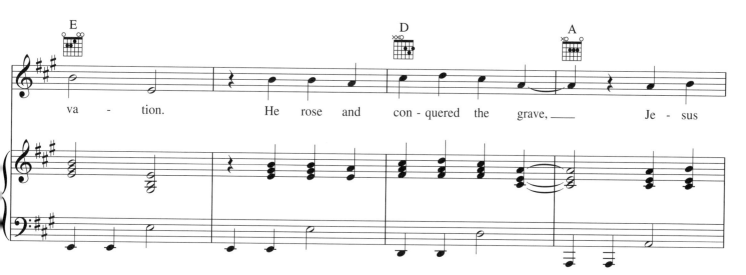

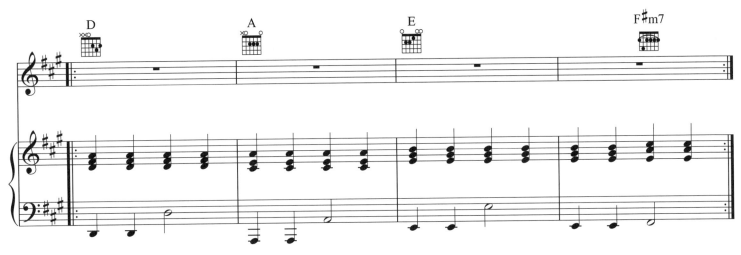

Shine your light and let the whole world ___ see. Sing- in'

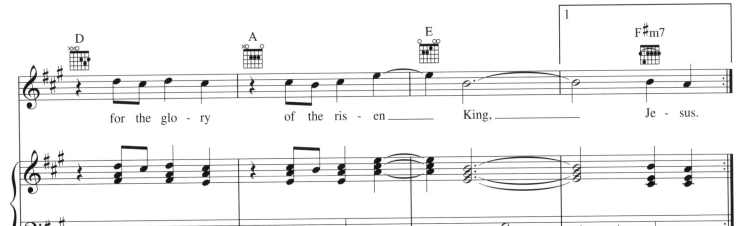

for the glo - ry of the ris - en ___ King, ___ Je - sus.

___ Sav - ior, He can move the moun - tains.

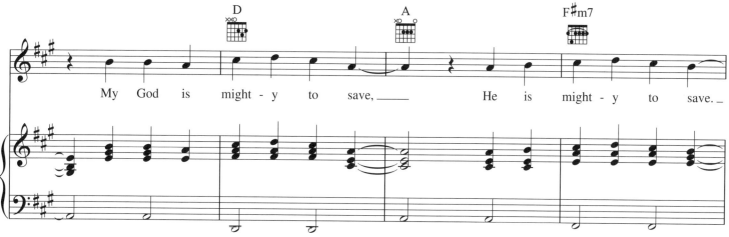

My God is might-y to save, ___ He is might-y to save. ___

___ For - ev - er, Au -thor of sal - va - tion.

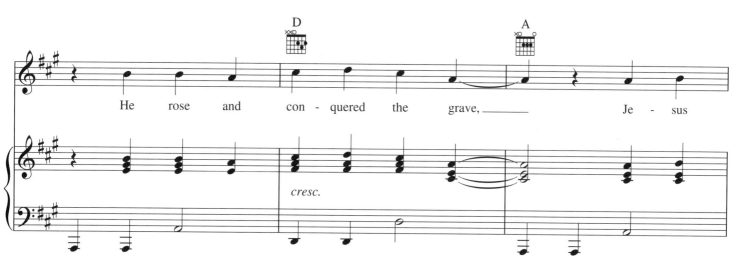

He rose and con - quered the grave, ___ Je - sus

con - quered the grave. ___ Sav - ior, He can move the

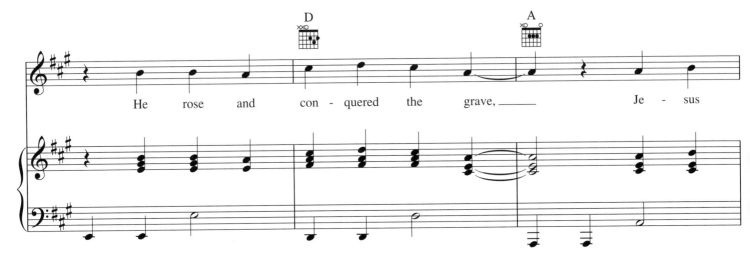

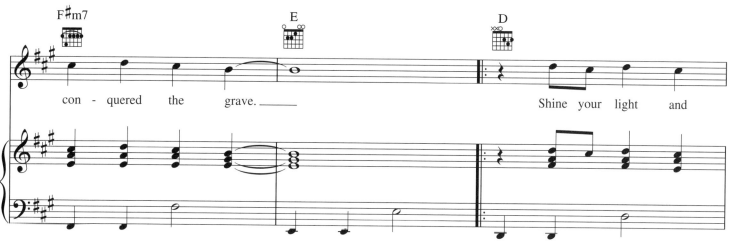

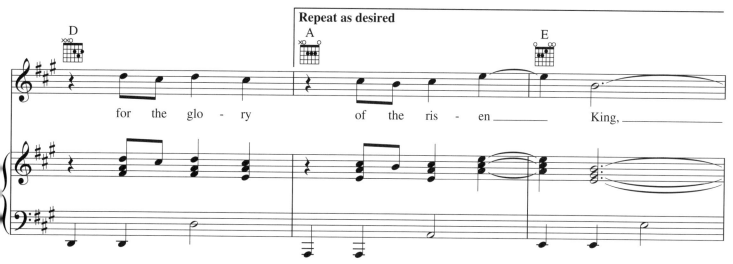

OUR GOD

Words and Music by JONAS MYRIN,
CHRIS TOMLIN, MATT REDMAN
and JESSE REEVES

With power

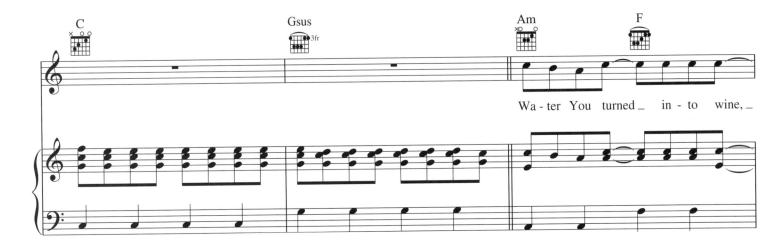

Wa - ter You turned _ in - to wine,

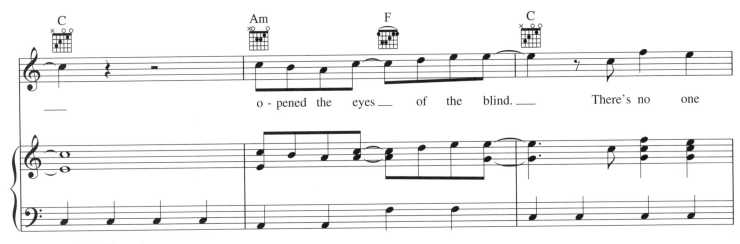

o - pened the eyes _ of the blind. _ There's no one

Recorded a half step lower.

like You, _ none like _____ You. _____

In - to the dark - ness You shine, ___ out of the ash - es we rise. _

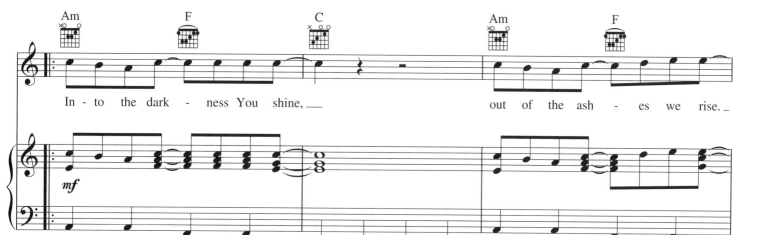

___ There's no one like You, _ none like ___

___ You. _____ Our God is great - er,

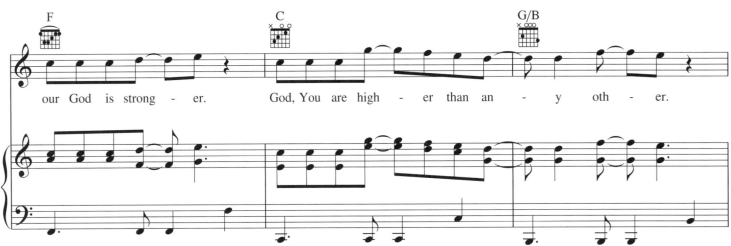

our God is strong - er. God, You are high - er than an - y oth - er.

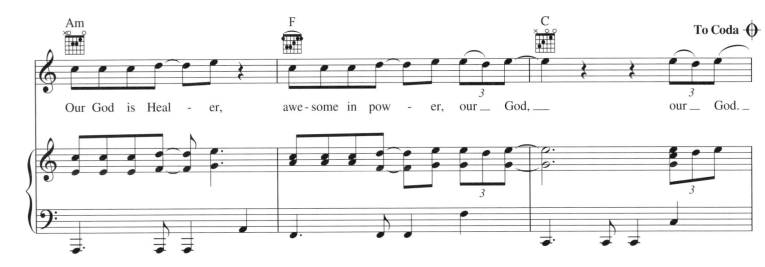

Our God is Heal - er, awe - some in pow - er, our __ God, __ our __ God. __

To Coda ⊕

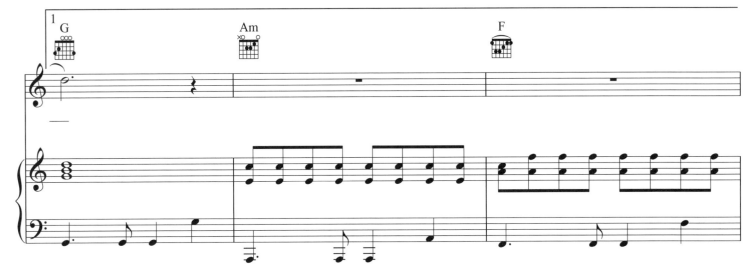

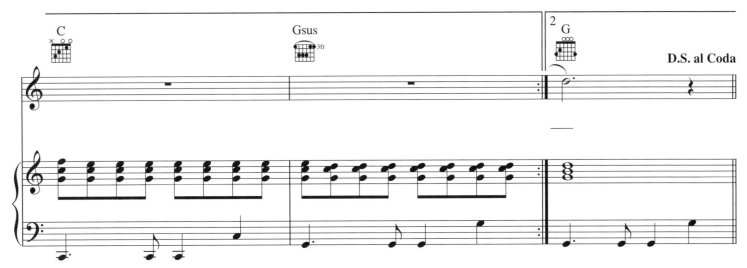

D.S. al Coda

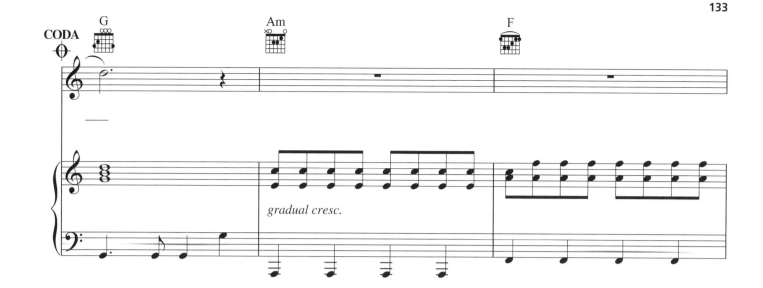

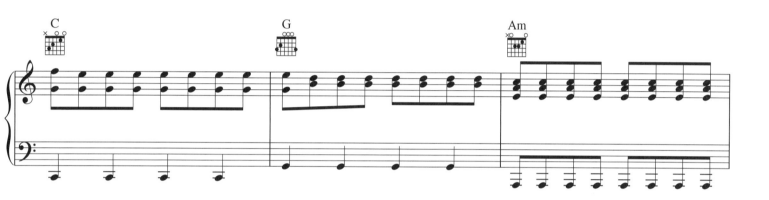

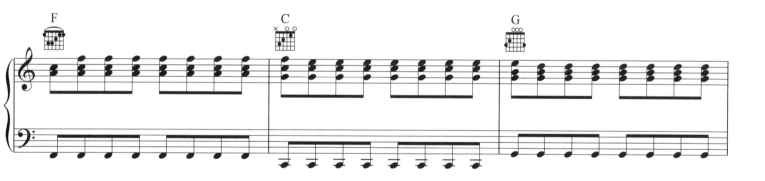

And if our God is for us, then who could ev - er stop us? And if our God is with us,

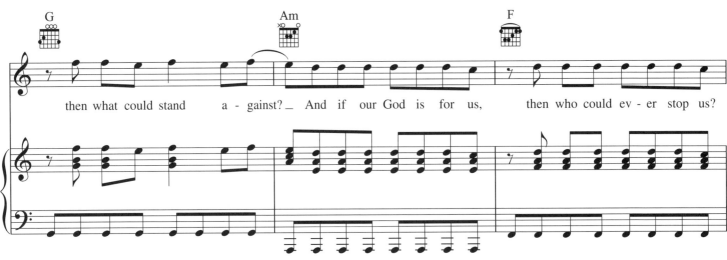

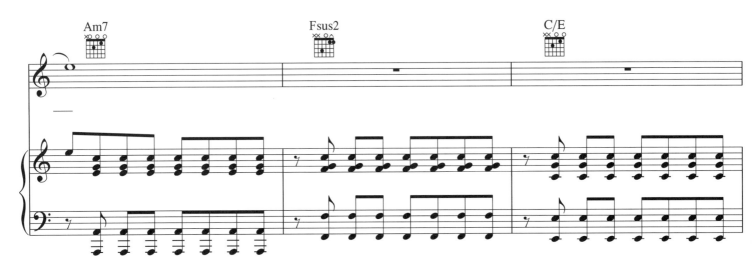

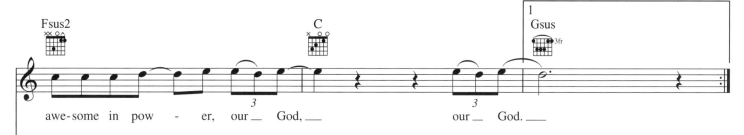

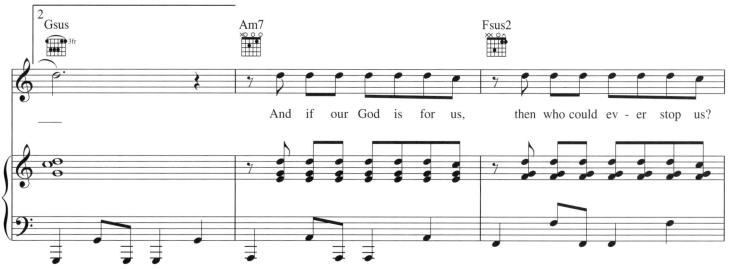

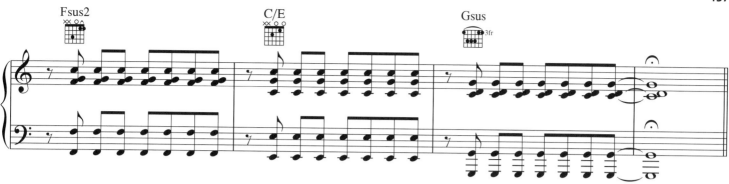

Our God is great-er, our God is strong-er. God, You are high-er than an-

-y oth-er. Our God is Heal-er, awe-some in pow-er, our_ God,_

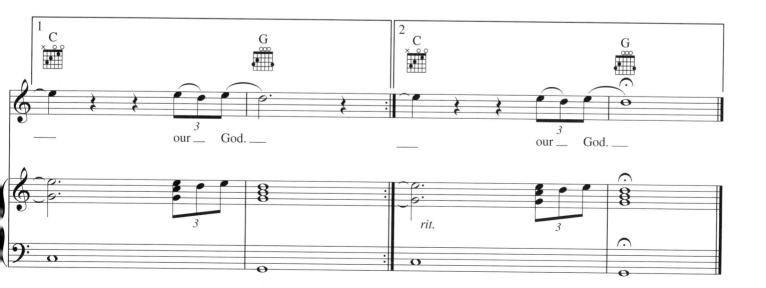

_ our_ God._ _ our_ God._

OUR GOD SAVES

Words and Music by PAUL BALOCHE
and BRENTON BROWN

-geth - er   to   lift   up   Your ___ name,   to   call   on   our ___

___ Sav - ior,   to   fall   on   Your ___ grace.

In   the   name   of   the ___

___ grace.   Hear   the   joy - ful ___ sound ___ of   our   of - fer - ing, ___   as   Your

saints bow down, as Your peo - ple sing. We will rise with You, lift - ed

on Your wings, and the world will see that our God

saves, our God saves.

There is hope in Your

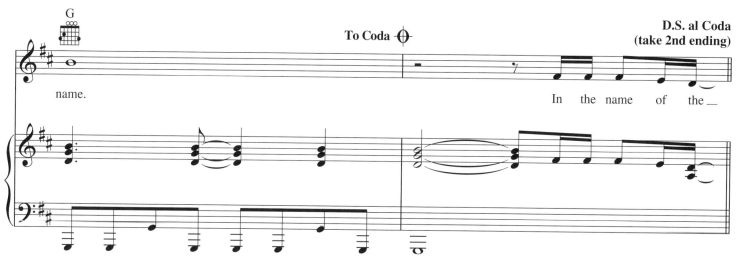

name.

To Coda

D.S. al Coda
(take 2nd ending)

In the name of the __

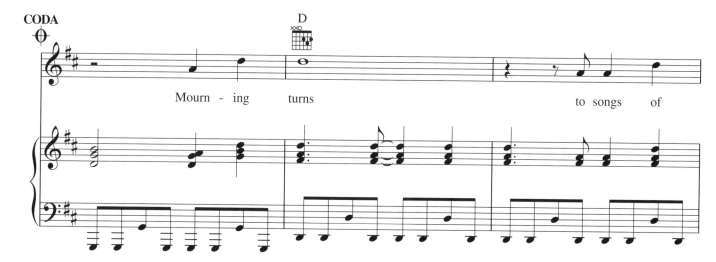

CODA

Mourn - ing turns

to songs of

praise.

Our God saves,

our God saves.

Yeah. _____

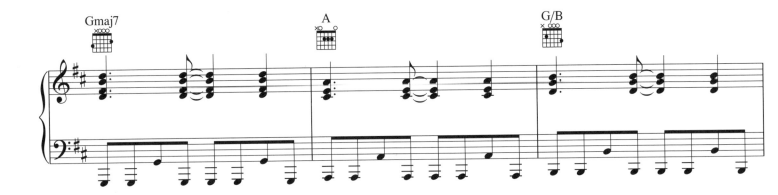

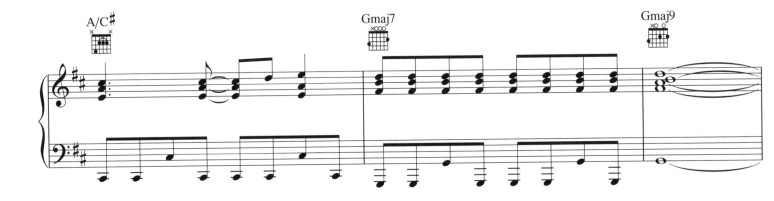

Hear the joy - ful __ sound __ of our of - fer - ing, __ as Your

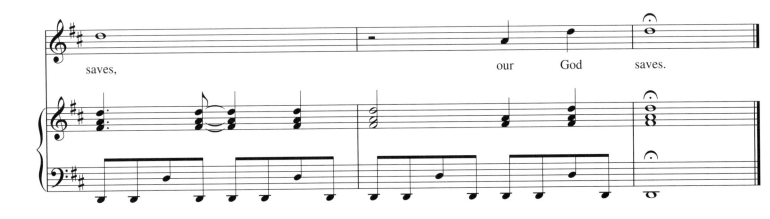

REVELATION SONG

Words and Music by
JENNIE LEE RIDDLE

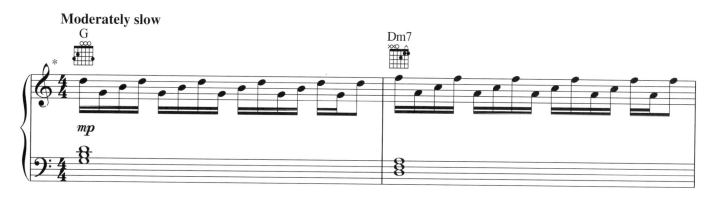

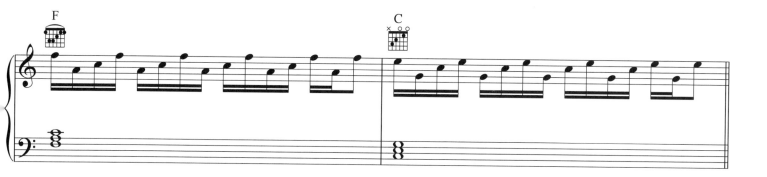

Wor - thy is the Lamb who was slain. Ho - ly, ho - ly is He._

Recorded a half step lower.

Sing a new song to ___ Him who sits on

Heav-en's mer - cy seat. ___

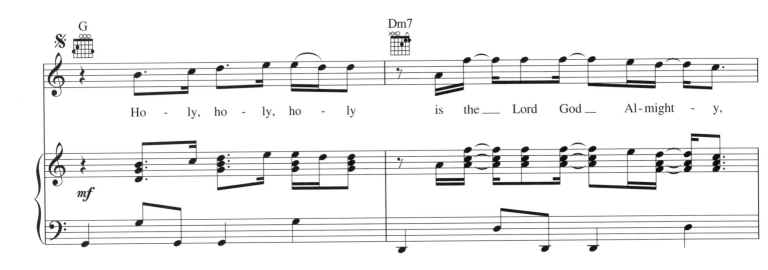

Ho - ly, ho - ly, ho - ly is the ___ Lord God ___ Al-might - y,

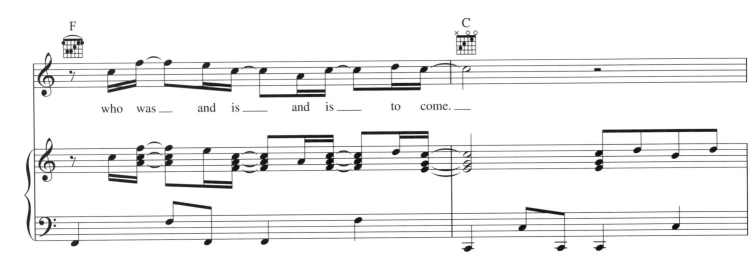

who was ___ and is ___ and is ___ to come. ___

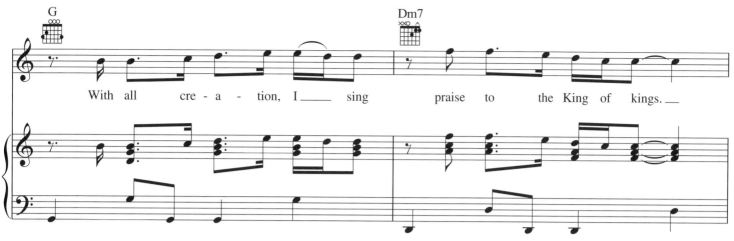

With all cre-a-tion, I sing praise to the King of kings.

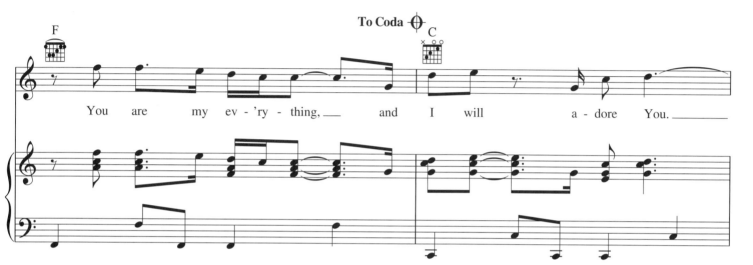

You are my ev-'ry-thing, and I will a-dore You.

Yeah, I will a-dore You.

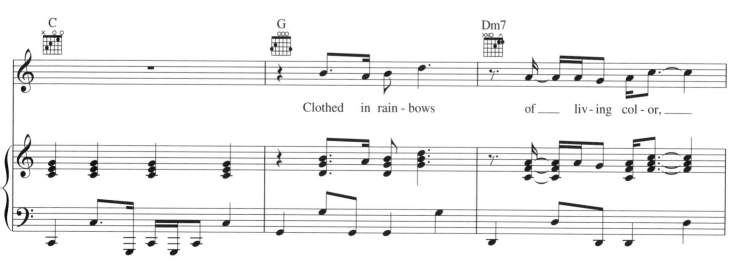

Clothed in rain-bows of living col-or,

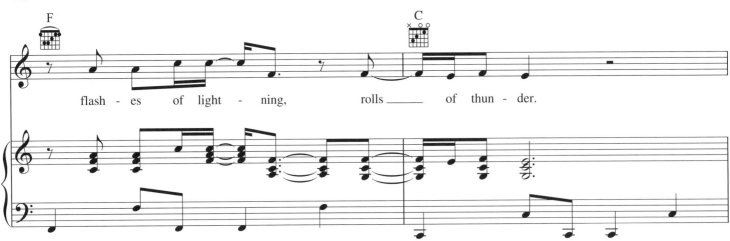

flash - es of light - ning, rolls ___ of thun - der.

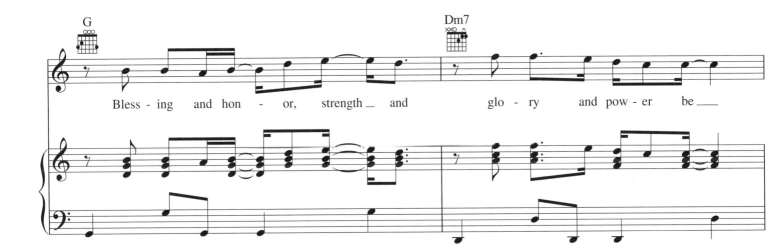

Bless - ing and hon - or, strength __ and glo - ry and pow - er be __

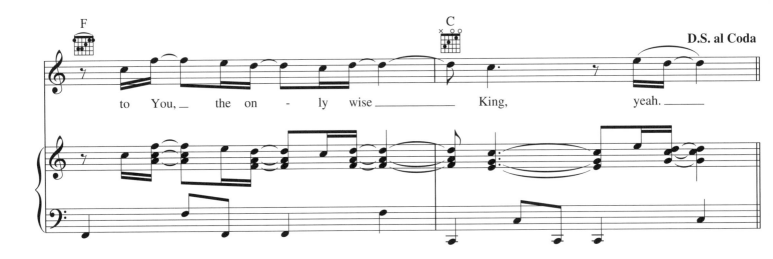

D.S. al Coda

to You, __ the on - ly wise _____ King, yeah. _____

I will a - dore You. (Ho - ly, __ ho - ly. _____

You are __ ho - ly.) _____ Filled with won - der,

awe - struck won - der, at the men - tion of __ Your __ name.

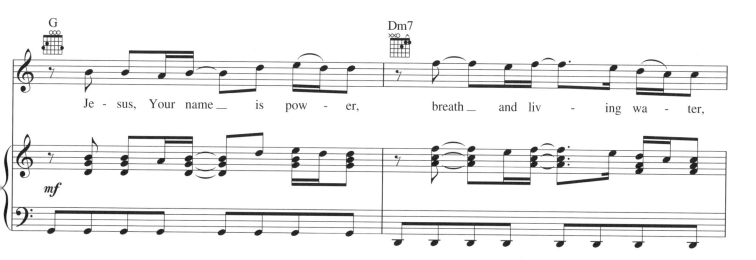

Je - sus, Your name __ is pow - er, breath __ and liv - ing wa - ter,

such __ a mar - v'lous mys - ter - y, _____ yeah. _____

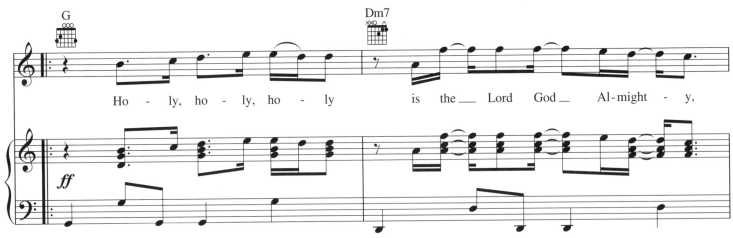

Ho - ly, ho - ly, ho - ly is the __ Lord God __ Al-might - y,

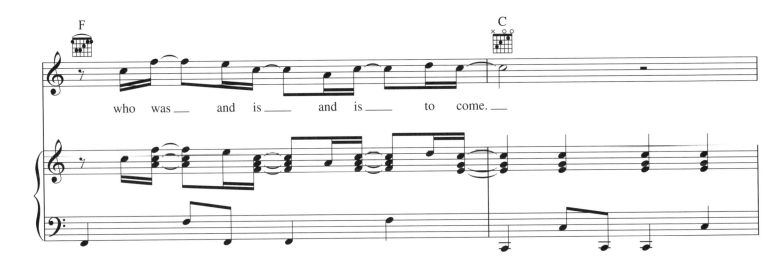

who was __ and is __ and is __ to come. __

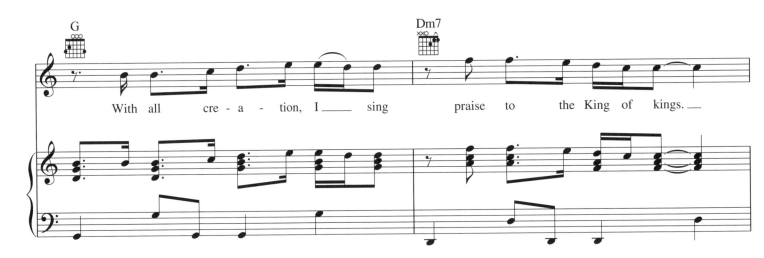

With all cre - a - tion, I __ sing praise to the King of kings. __

You are my ev - 'ry - thing, __ and I will a - dore You.

SING, SING, SING

Words and Music by CHRIS TOMLIN,
JESSE REEVES, DANIEL CARSON,
TRAVIS NUNN and MATT GILDER

Moderately fast

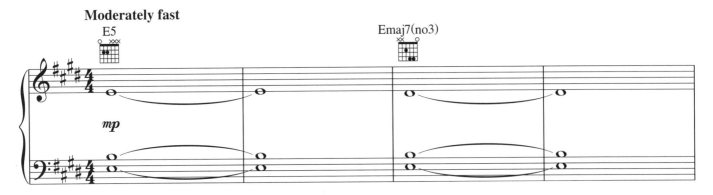

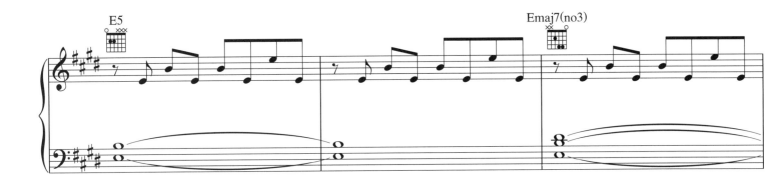

Sing, sing, sing, ___ and make mu-

What's not to love _

_ a - bout _ You? Heav - en and earth _ a - dore _ You.

C#m7

Kings _ and king - doms bow _ down. _____ Son of God, _

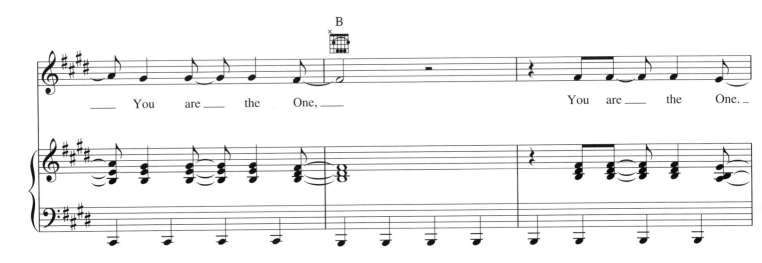

_ You are _ the One, _ You are _ the One. _

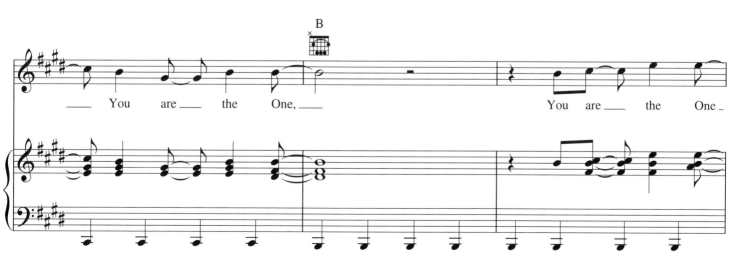

Kings __ and king - doms bow __ down. _____ Son of God, _

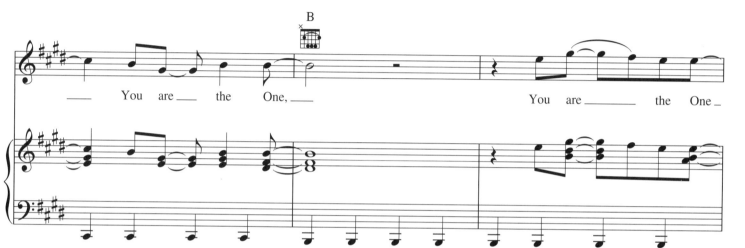

__ You are __ the One, ____ You are _____ the One _

__ we're liv - ing for. _____

__ Sing, sing, sing, ___ and make mu -

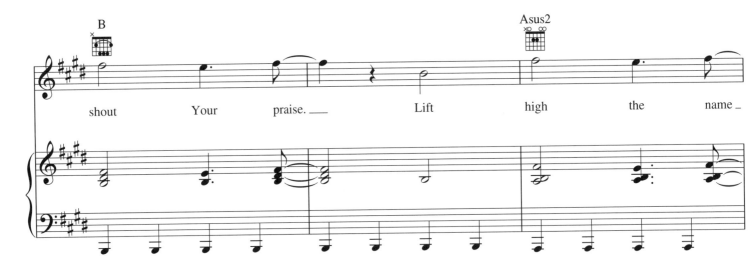

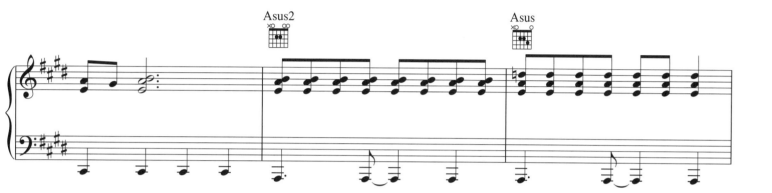

Sing, sing, sing, _____ and make mu - sic with __ the heav -

- ens. Sing, sing, sing, _____ grate -

-ful that ___ You hear ___ us. We shout Your praise. ___

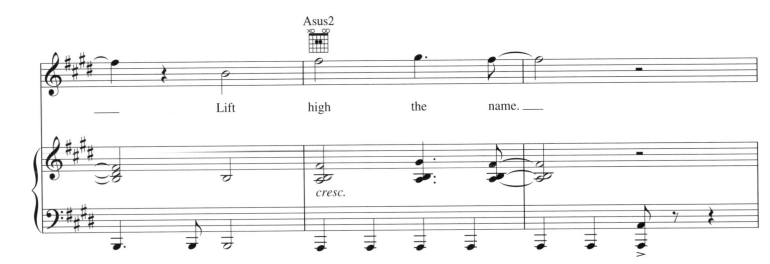

___ Lift high the name. ___

Sing, sing, sing, ___ and make mu - sic with ___ the heav -

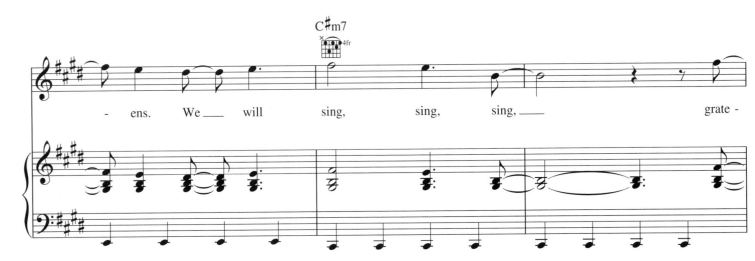

-ens. We ___ will sing, sing, sing, ___ grate -

ful that ___ You hear ___ us. We shout Your praise. _

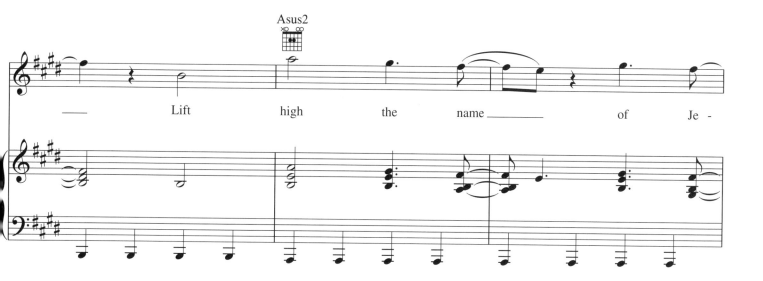

___ Lift high the name _____ of Je -

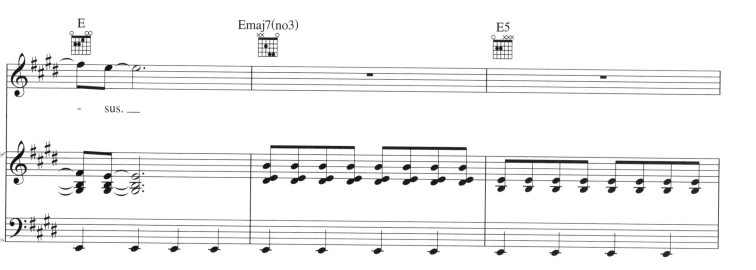

\- sus. __

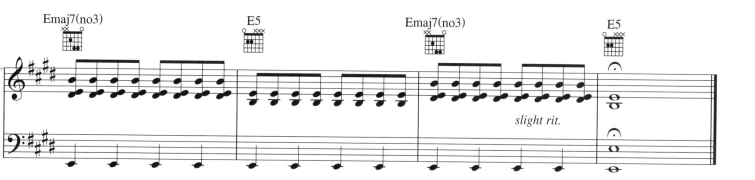

slight rit.

SING TO THE KING

Words and Music by
BILLY JAMES FOOTE

Life and salvation His empire shall bring,
We'll join in singing with all the redeemed,

and joy to the nations when
'cause Satan is vanquished when and

1

Je - sus is King.
Je - sus is King.

2, 3

Come, let us sing a song, a

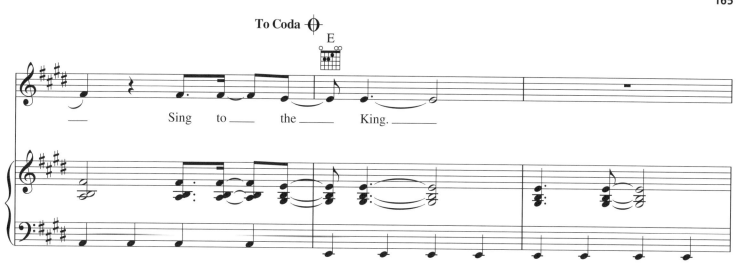

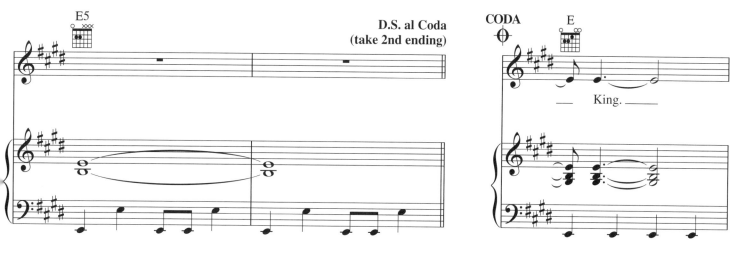

SPEAK O LORD

Words and Music by STUART TOWNEND
and KEITH GETTY

Prayerfully

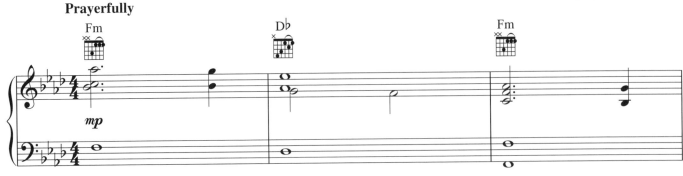

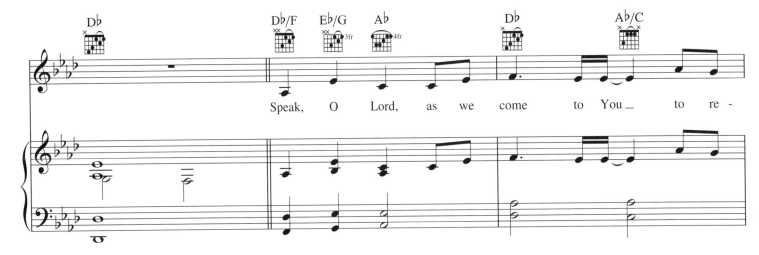

Speak, O Lord, as we come to You _ to re-

ceive the food _ of Your ho - ly Word. _ Take Your truth, plant it

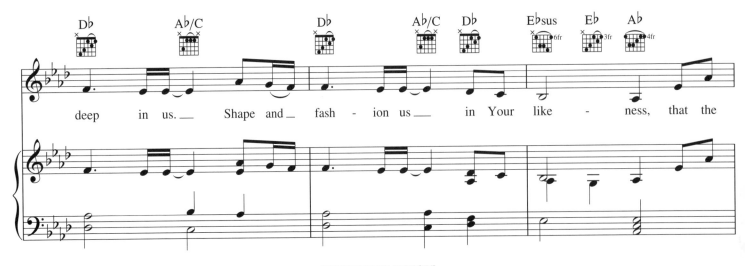

deep in us. _ Shape and _ fash - ion us _ in Your like - ness, that the

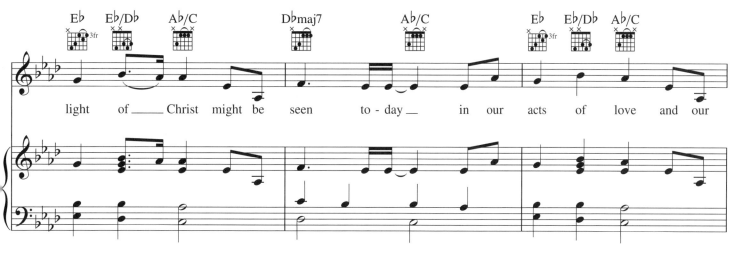

light of ___ Christ might be seen to-day __ in our acts of love and our

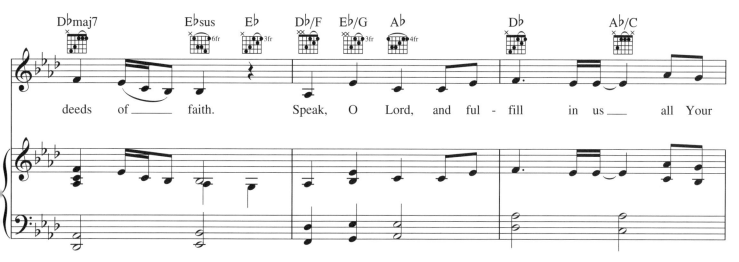

deeds of ___ faith. Speak, O Lord, and ful - fill in us __ all Your

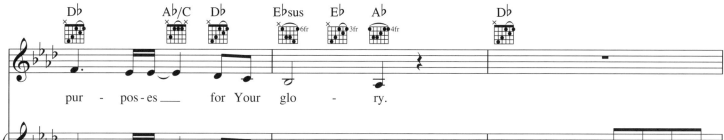

pur - pos - es __ for Your glo - ry.

Teach us, Lord, full o - be - di - ence, __ ho - ly
Speak, O Lord, and re - new our minds. __ Help us

rev - er - ence,___ true hu - mil - i - ty.___ Test our thoughts and our
grasp the heights _ of Your plans for us.___ Truths un - changed from the

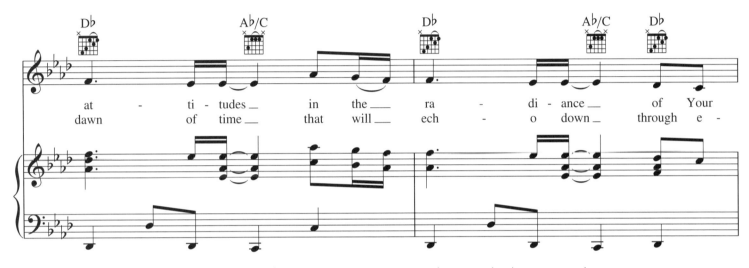

at - ti - tudes _ in the ___ ra - di - ance ___ of Your
dawn of time __ that will ___ ech - o down _ through e -

pu - ri - ty.___ Cause our faith to _____ rise, cause our
ter - ni - ty.___ And by grace we'll ___ stand on Your

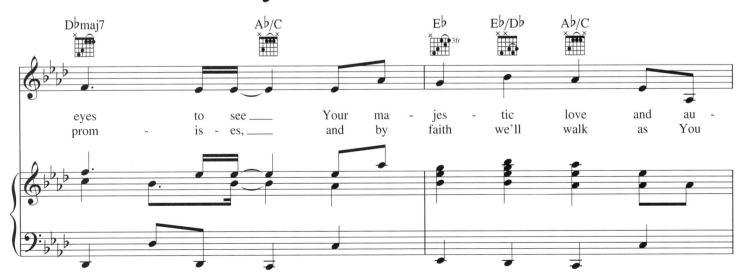

eyes to see ___ Your ma - jes - tic love and au -
prom - is - es, ___ and by faith we'll walk as You

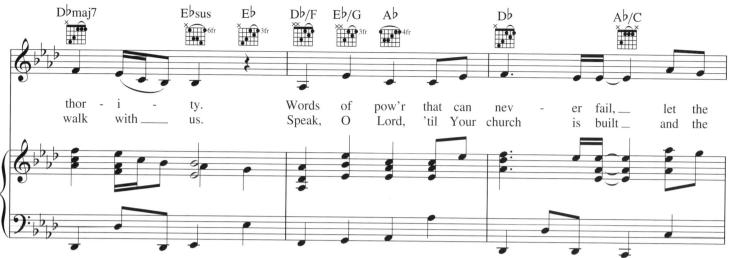

thor - i - ty.
walk with us.

Words of pow'r that can nev - er fail, let the
Speak, O Lord, 'til Your church is built and the

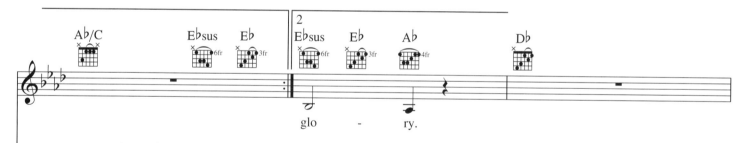

truth pre - vail o - ver un - be - lief.
earth is filled with Your

glo - ry.

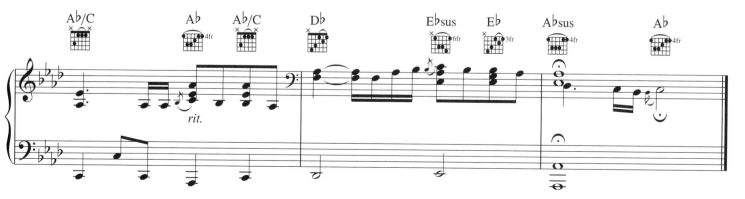

TODAY IS THE DAY

Words and Music by LINCOLN BREWSTER
and PAUL BALOCHE

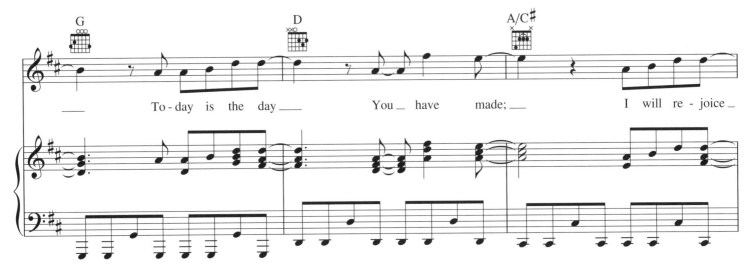

to - mor - row, I'm trust-ing in what _ You say. _ To - day is the day. _

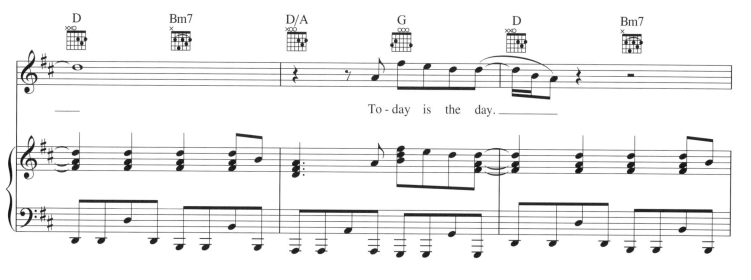

To - day is the day. _____

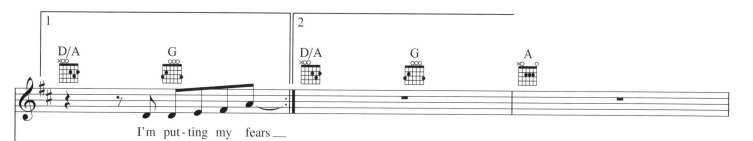

I'm put-ting my fears _

Guitar solo ad lib.

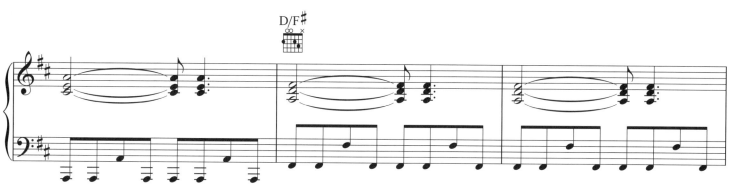

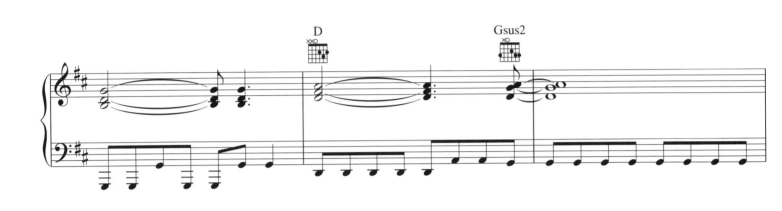

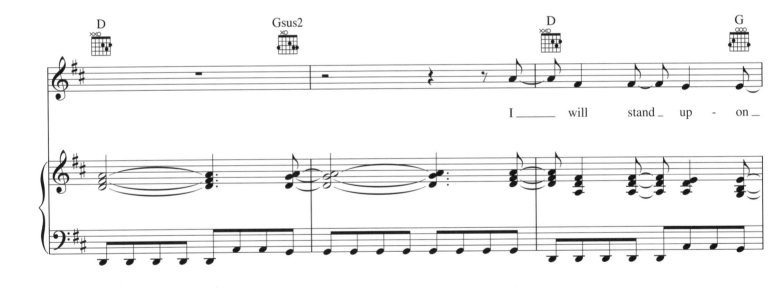

I _____ will stand _ up - on _

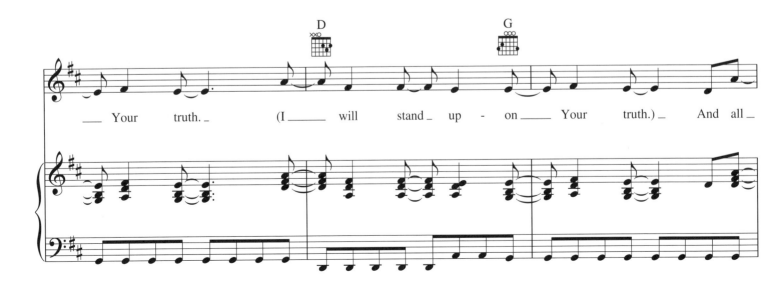

_____ Your truth. _ (I _____ will stand _ up - on _____ Your truth.) _ And all _

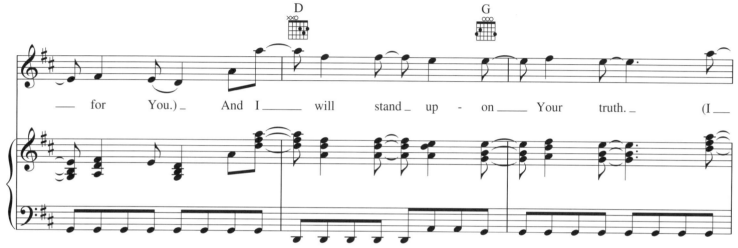

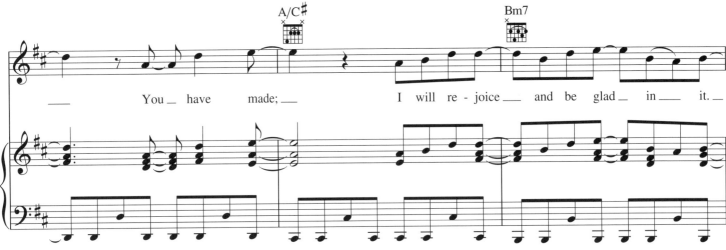

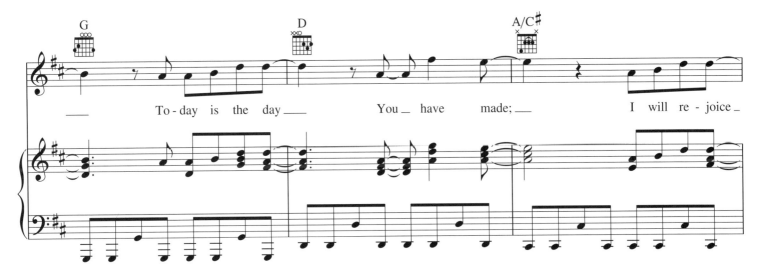

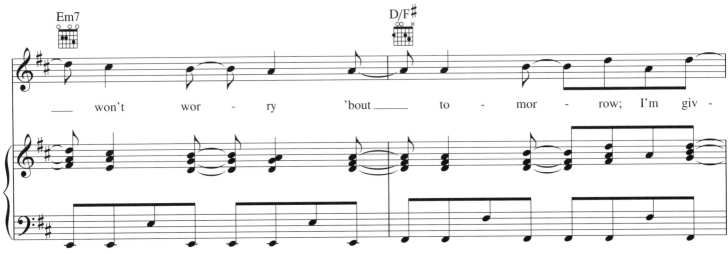

-ing You__ my fears__ and sor - rows. Where __

__ You lead__ me, I____ will fol - low. I'm trust-ing in what__ You say.__

__ To - day is the day. ____ To - day is the day. __

To - day is the day. ____

YOU ALONE CAN RESCUE

Words and Music by JONAS MYRIN
and MATT REDMAN

Recorded a half step lower.

still. Who, O Lord, could save them- selves,

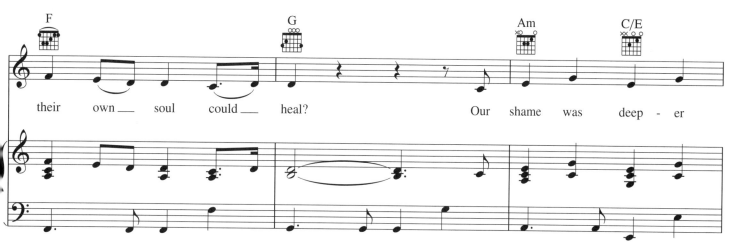

their own ___ soul could ___ heal? Our shame was deep - er

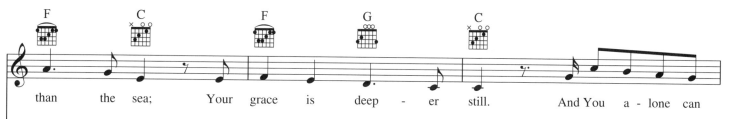

than the sea; Your grace is deep - er still. And You a - lone can

res - cue, You a - lone can save. You a - lone can lift us from ___ the grave. ___

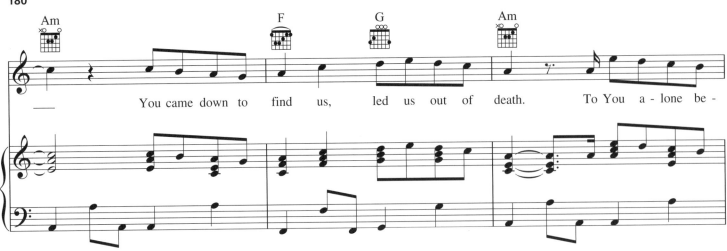

You came down to find us, led us out of death. To You a-lone be-

longs the high - est praise. ___

You, O Lord, have made a way; the great di - vide You ___

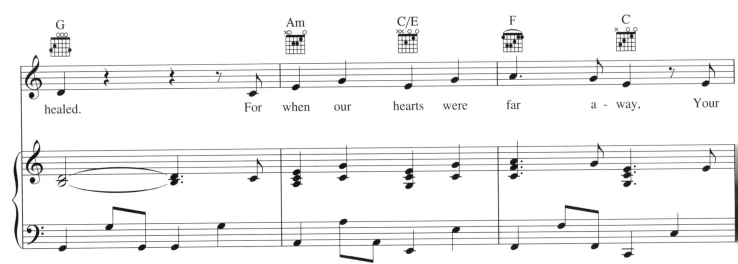

healed. For when our hearts were far a - way, Your

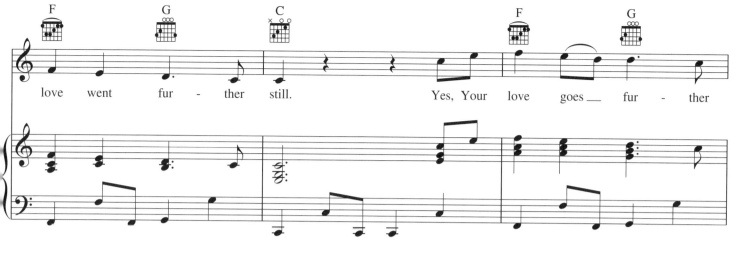

love went fur - ther still. Yes, Your love goes ___ fur - ther

still. And You a - lone can res - cue, You a - lone can save. You a - lone can

cresc.

f

lift us from ___ the grave. ___ You came down to find us, led us out of

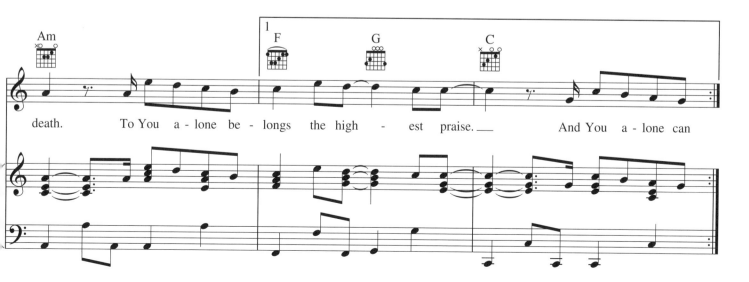

death. To You a - lone be - longs the high - est praise. ___ And You a - lone can

longs the high - est praise. __ To You a - lone be - longs the high - est praise. __

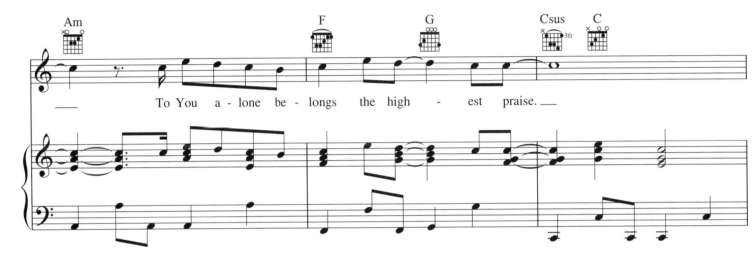

__ To You a - lone be - longs the high - est praise. __

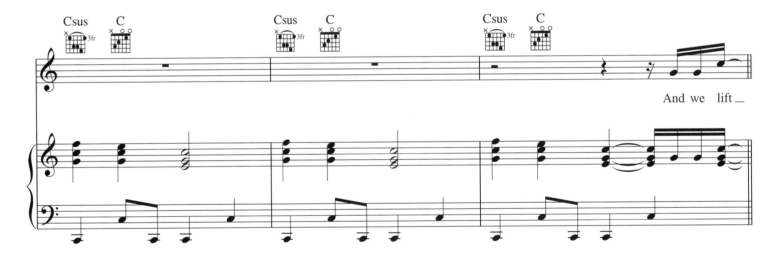

And we lift __

__ up our eyes, lift __ up our eyes to the giv - er of life. We lift __

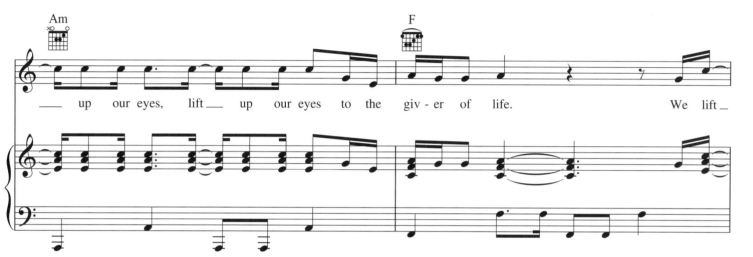

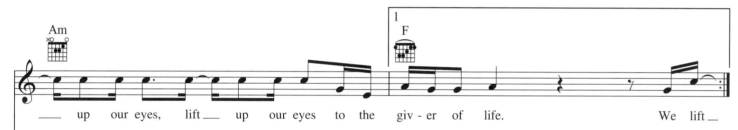

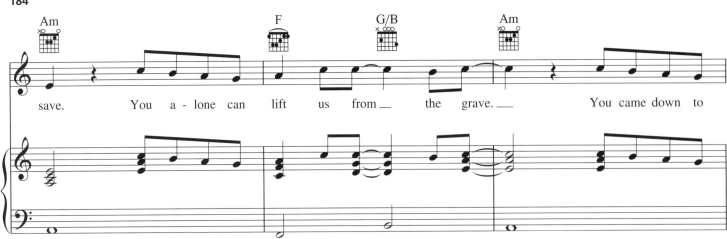

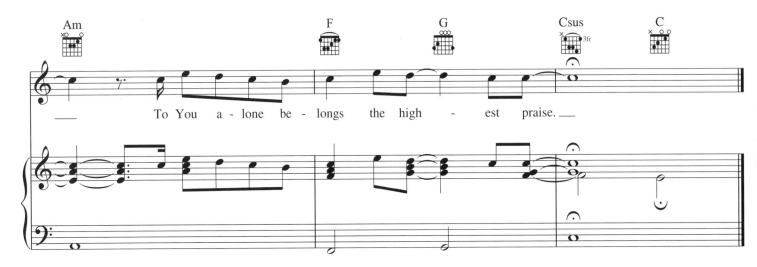

YOU ARE GOD ALONE
(not a god)

Words and Music by BILLY J. FOOTE
and CINDY FOOTE

In a slow two

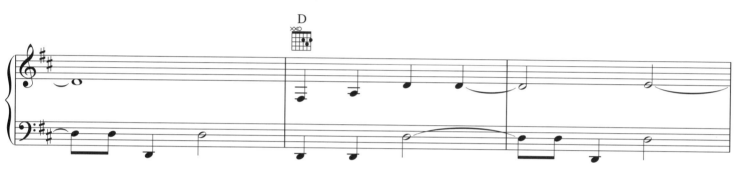

You are not a

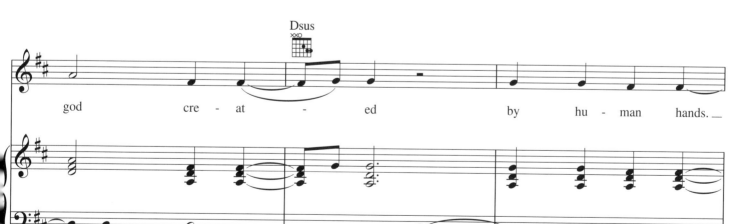

god cre - at - ed by hu - man hands. __

* *Recorded a half step lower.*

You are not a god de-pend - ent on

an - y mor-tal man.____ You are not a god in need____

____ of _____ an - y - thing we can give.____ By Your

plan, that's just the way ___ it is. _____

You are God a - lone.

And right now, in the good times and bad,

You are on Your throne, and

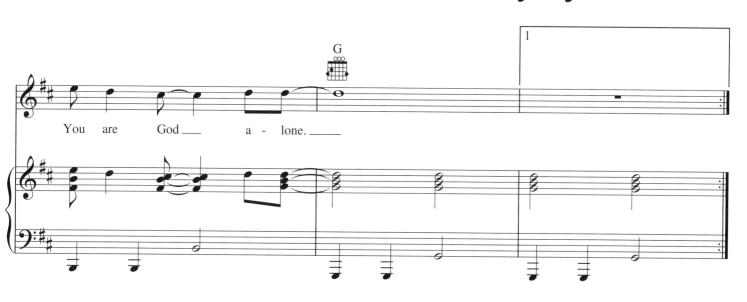

You are God a - lone.

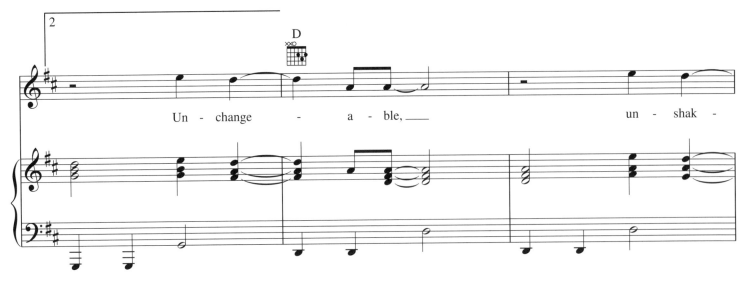

Un - change - - a - ble, ___ un - shak -

- a - ble, ___ un - stop - pa - ble, ___

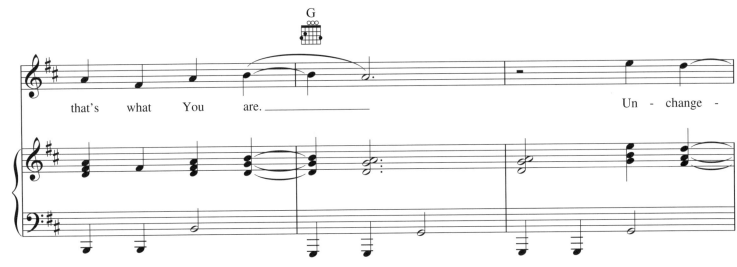

that's what You are. _____ Un - change -

- a - ble, ___ un - shak - a - ble, ___

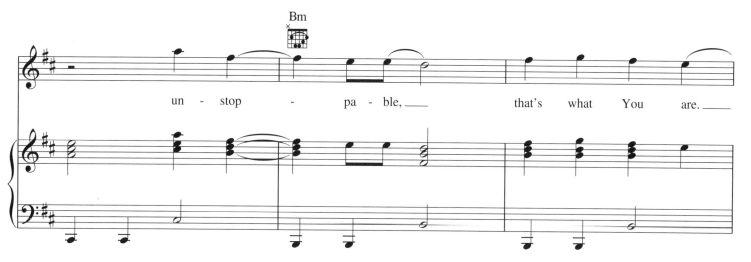

un - stop - pa - ble, _____ that's what You are. _____

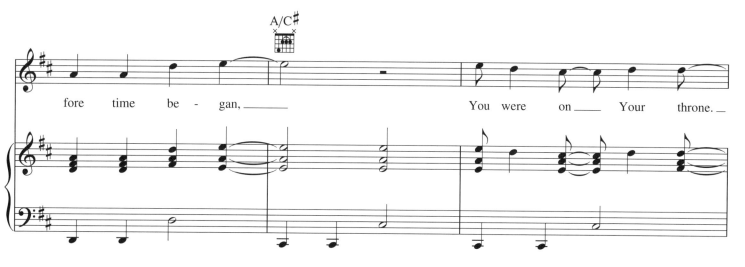

_____ You are God _____ a - lone. _____ From be -

fore time be - gan, _____ You were on _____ Your throne. _

_____ You are God _____ a - lone. _____

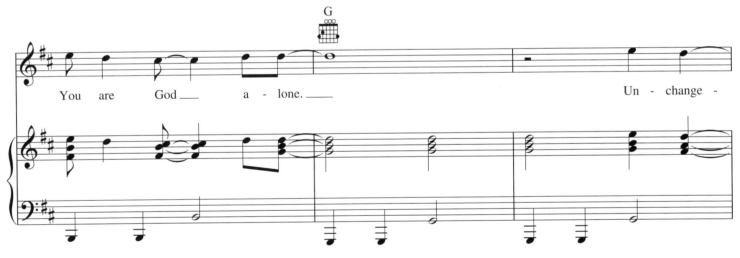

un - stop - pa - ble, ___ that's what You are. ___

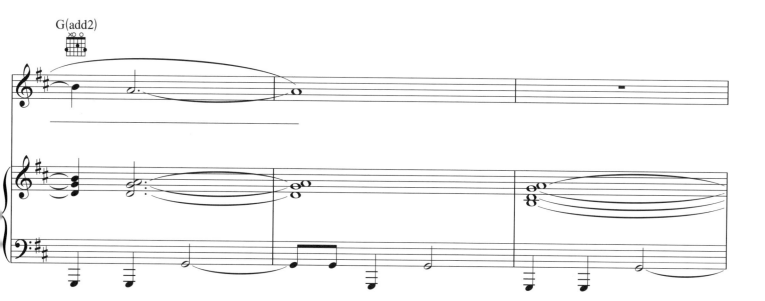

Repeat and Fade

Optional Ending

YOU, YOU ARE GOD

Words and Music by
MICHAEL WALKER BEACH

bring to You _ an of - fer - ing. _ I have to ask _ my - self _
cause You gave _ Your life _ for me, _ You cru - ci - fied _ Your Son _

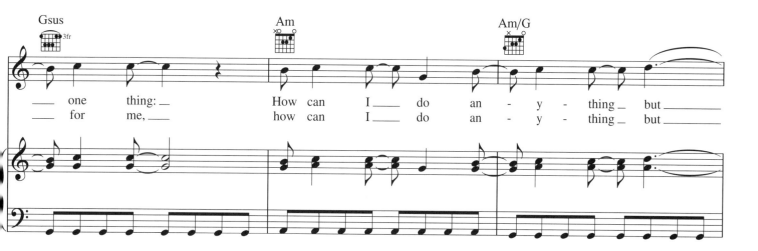

_ one thing: _ How can I _ do an - y - thing _ but _
_ for me, _ how can I _ do an - y - thing _ but _

_ praise? _
_ praise? _ I _ praise. _
I _ praise. _

_ You, You, You are God, _ You are Lord, _
(D.S.) _

You are all ___ I'm liv-ing for. ___ You are King ___

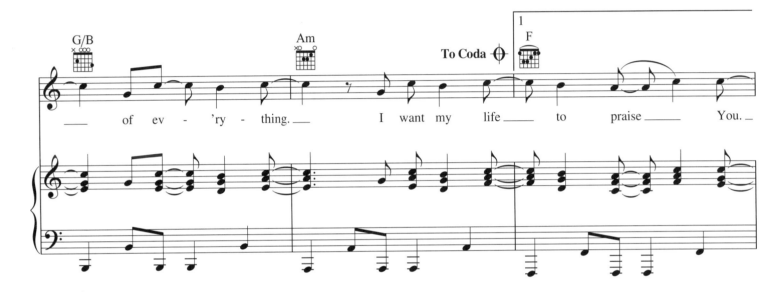

___ of ev-'ry-thing. ___ I want my life ___ to praise ___ You. ___

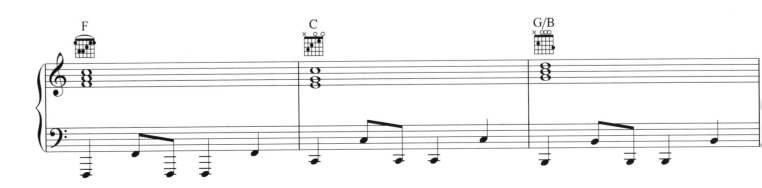

to praise _____ You. ___

D.S. al Coda

to praise _____ You. ___

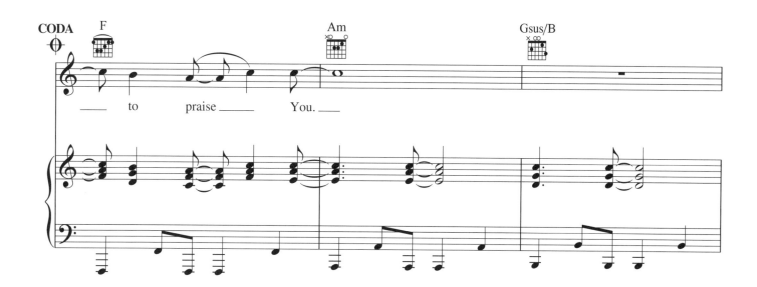

You, You are God, You are Lord, You are all

I'm liv - ing for. You are King of ev - 'ry - thing.

I want my life to praise You. to praise You.

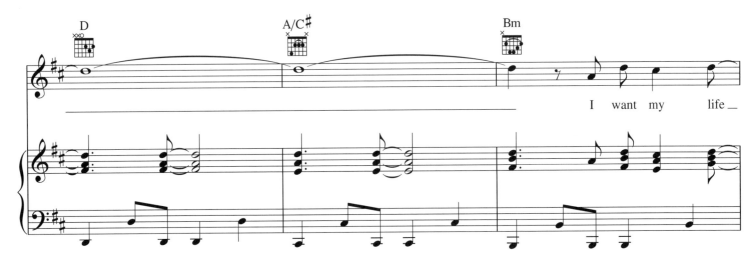

I want my life

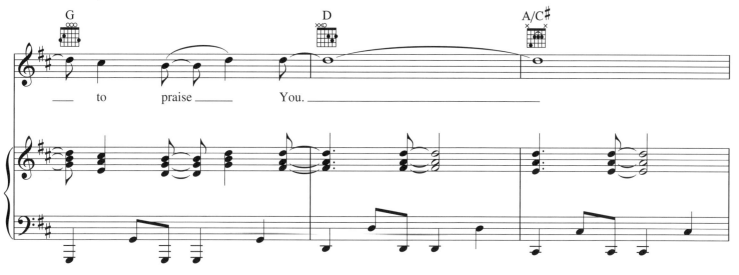

to praise You.

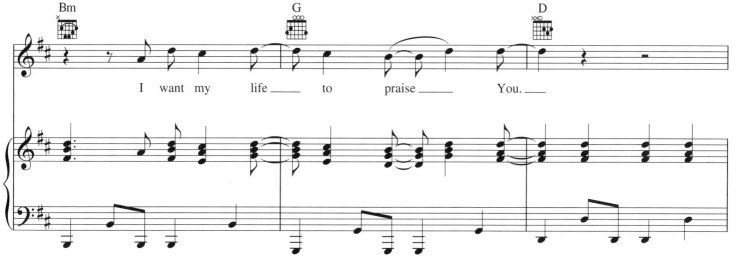

I want my life to praise You.

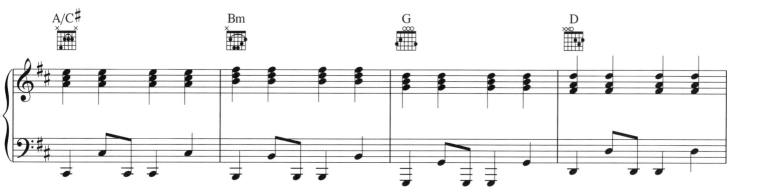

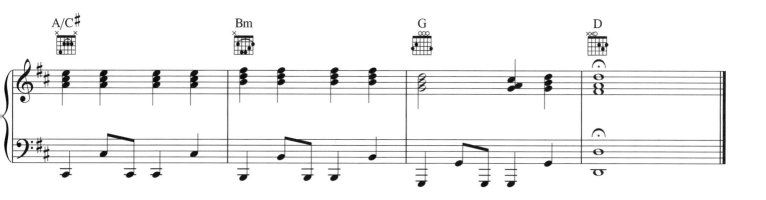

YOUR LOVE NEVER FAILS

Words and Music by ANTHONY SKINNER
and CHRIS McCLARNEY

Moderate Pop feel

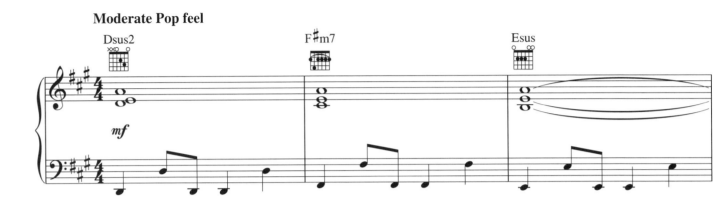

Noth - ing ___ can

sep - a - rate. E - ven if I ran a - way, Your _

_ love nev - er fails. ___ Mm. ___

I know I __ still make mis - takes, _ but

You have new mer - cy for me ev - 'ry day, 'cause Your __ love nev - er fails. _

the o - ceans rage, __ I don't have __ to be a - fraid, __

be - cause I know that __ You love me, __ and Your __

__ love nev - er fails. __

The wind is strong __ and the

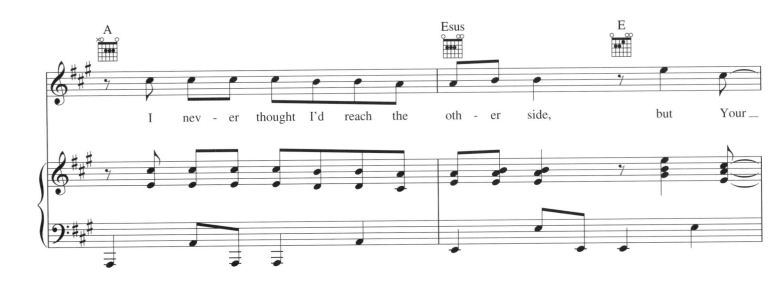

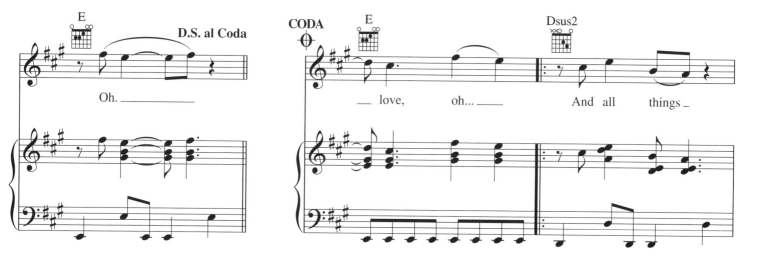

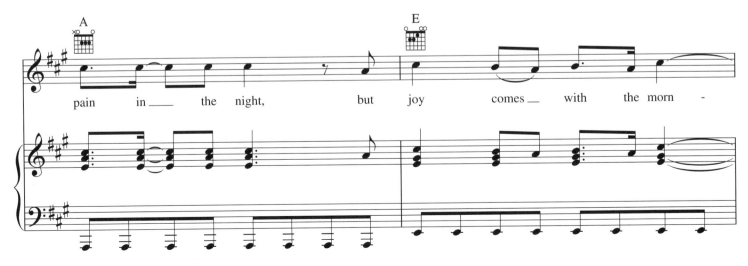

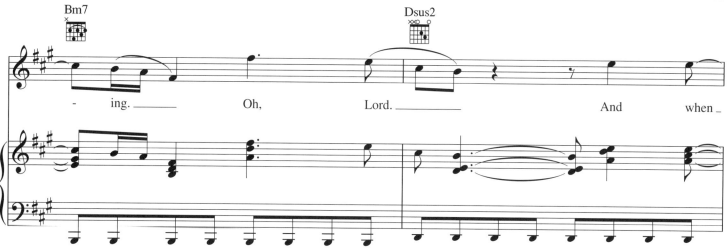

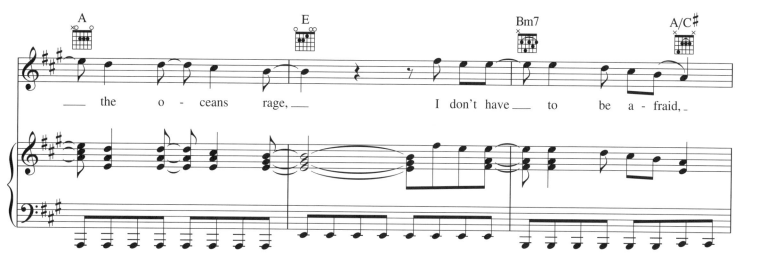

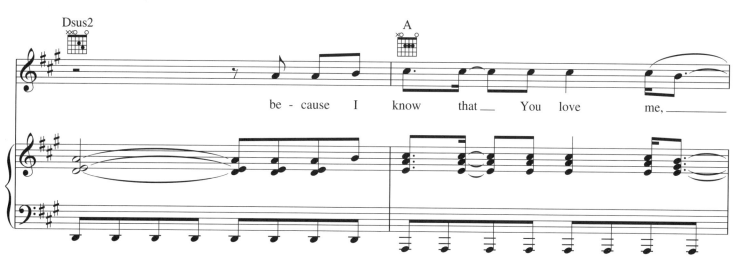

and Your ___ love nev - er fails. ___

Your love ___ nev - er fails, Your love nev - er fails. ___

All things
all things } work to - geth - er for my good. ___

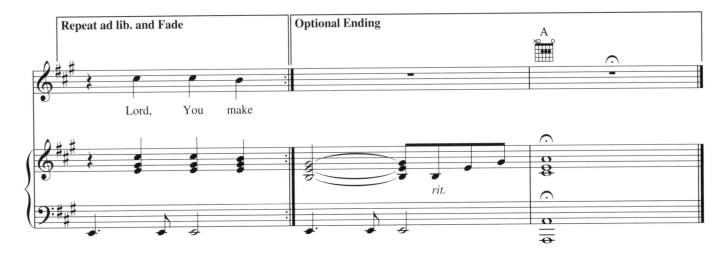

Repeat ad lib. and Fade

Lord, You make

Optional Ending

rit.